TWENTIETH CENTURY INTERPRETATIONS

OF

A FAREWELL TO ARMS

A Collection of Critical Essays

Edited by

JAY GELLENS

Prentice-Hall, Inc.   A SPECTRUM BOOK *Englewood Cliffs, N. J.*

Current printing (last number):
10   9   8   7   6   5   4   3   2   1

PRENTICE-HALL INTERNATIONAL, INC. (*London*)
PRENTICE-HALL OF AUSTRALIA, PTY. LTD. (*Sydney*)
PRENTICE-HALL OF CANADA, LTD. (*Toronto*)
PRENTICE-HALL OF INDIA PRIVATE LIMITED (*New Delhi*)
PRENTICE-HALL OF JAPAN, INC. (*Tokyo*)

Contents

iii

Introduction

by Jay Gellens

A Farewell to Arms, Hemingway's second novel and first significant popular success, was published in 1929, at the end of a ten-year postwar binge of jazz and prohibition, big business and organized crime, the League of Nations and the rise of fascism. The country was sexually liberated, utterly bored, and on the brink of economic disaster. Coming at that time, the book appealed most to an appetite for adventure, offering an innocent love affair threatened and deepened by a real enemy; but an enemy from which all readers could feel safe, for the war, though still available to recollection, had faded to a remote, unbelievable fantasy of heroics. Malcolm Cowley patronized the book as the farewell "to a period, an attitude—the simple standards of wartime," and moralized on Hemingway's responsibility to deal with the stuff of daily life, the emotions "less violently stimulated in a world at peace." [1] Robert Penn Warren, on the other hand, later praised Hemingway's decision to "cut back to the beginning of the process, to the moment that . . . held within itself the explanation of the subsequent process." [2]

Contemporary critics in general certified the popular enthusiasm for it. They applauded its stylistic achievement, at once "bluff, masculine, hard-boiled, apparently insensitive . . . ," yet enabling "a very vivid and sometimes poignant picture of the life Hemingway knows." They also admired the "vividly realized scenes," the "brilliantly authentic dialogue," and concluded that Hemingway's "genius declares itself in the perfection of detail." [3] In particular, Arnold Bennett found it "utterly free of any sentimentality," yet "imbued through and through with genuine sentiment," while Bernard De Voto argued that

---

[1] Malcolm Cowley, "Review of A Farewell to Arms," *New York Herald Tribune (Books),* October 6, 1929, pp. 1, 16.

[2] Robert Penn Warren, "Hemingway," *Selected Essays* (New York: Random House, Inc., 1954), p. 81.

[3] J. B. Priestly, *Now and Then* 34 (Winter 1929): 1–12; Henry Hazlitt, *New York Sun,* September 28, 1929, p. 38; John Dos Passos, *New Masses* 5 (December 1, 1929), 1092; Edgar Johnson, "Farewell the Separate Peace: The Rejections of Ernest Hemingway," *Sewanee Review* 48 (July–September 1940): 298–300.

Hemingway "for the first time, justifies his despair and gives it the dignity of a tragic emotion." [4]

Later critics, notably Edmund Wilson, have sometimes demurred. Wilson sees in Catherine and Frederic "innocent victims with no relation to the forces that torment them." Examined closely, they offer "merely an idealized relationship, the abstractions of a lyric emotion." [5] D. S. Savage, dismissing the entire Hemingway scene as an "eviscerated, chaotic world of futility and boredom, lit up with flashes of violent action," characterizes the Hemingway hero as a "creature without religion, morality, politics, culture, or history—without any of those aspects . . . of the distinctively human existence," and Hemingway himself as one who had "no coherent inner vision of human existence." [6] To Wyndham Lewis, Hemingway was "like an animal speaking." In a ferocious Swiftian tirade, he calls the Hemingway hero a "dull-witted, bovine, monosyllabic simpleton," the "voice of the folk, of the masses, cannon-fodder, cattle outside the slaughterhouse serenely chewing their cud, the people to whom things are done, in contrast to those who have executive will and intelligence." Hemingway has expressed with genius, Lewis states, the "soul of the dumb ox," which has a "penetrating beauty" like "the folk-song of the baboon, or of the 'Praying Mantis.' " [7]

More sympathetic critics, seeking to account for the novel's vivid sense of felt life, have preferred to locate it in a variety of conscious, often contradictory theoretical structures. Carlos Baker writes of the symbolism of Mountain and Plain;[8] Cowley, in a later study than that mentioned above, of nightmare and ritual.[9] Robert Penn Warren has isolated the aristocratic ethics of the Hemingway code,[10] and Cleanth Brooks has pioneered a belief in Hemingway's Christianity, grounding this, in a rather secular way, in the hero's persistent idealism, his perennial effort to generate significance, moral or otherwise,

---

[4] Arnold Bennett, *Evening Standard* (London), November 14, 1929; *Times* (London), November 15, 1929, p. 20; Clifton Fadiman, *Nation* 129 (October 30, 1929): 497–98; Bernard De Voto, "Review of *A Farewell to Arms,*" *Bookwise* 1 (November 1929): 5–9.

[5] Edmund Wilson, "Hemingway: Gauge of Morale," *The Wound and the Bow* (New York: Oxford University Press, 1947), pp. 214–42.

[6] D. S. Savage, *The Withered Branch: Six Studies in the Modern Novel* (London: Eyre & Spottiswoode, Ltd., 1950), pp. 23–43.

[7] Wyndham Lewis, *Men Without Art* (London: Cassell and Company, Ltd., 1934), pp. 17–40.

[8] Carlos Baker, *Hemingway: The Writer as Artist* (Princeton: Princeton University Press, 1956), pp. 94–116.

[9] Malcolm Cowley, "Introduction," *The Portable Hemingway* (New York: The Viking Press, Inc., 1944), pp. vii–xxiv.

[10] Warren, *Selected Essays,* pp. 80–118.

out of his habitual defiance of the Nada in experience.[11] Jean-Paul Sartre even compares Hemingway's style with that of Camus,[12] and, in this same vein, John Killinger undertakes to trace a rigorously pure Existentialism throughout the work, an attitude systematically antagonistic to all rituals and codes, to Christianity, and to symbolic constructs of any kind.[13]

Hemingway's position within the larger community of modern literature lies, perhaps, somewhere between Kafka and Camus. Hemingway's hero wastes no time in direct assaults on castles or courtrooms, nor is he willing, like Camus' Meursalt, to resign himself to a bleak, existential nightmare. His commitment to a secular code, in love, in war, in sports, in earning a living, is generally acknowledged. Hemingway, further, has not been willing to have it both ways like Conrad, who preserves, through his surrogate Marlow, a final ironic detachment from that "shadowy ideal of conduct" into whose embrace Lord Jim finally disappears—impressive, but always a little absurd. Hemingway's entire career is, ultimately, an unironic commitment to that ideal embrace.

Born in Oak Park, Illinois, in 1899, into the family of a middle-class doctor and a musical mother, Hemingway spent his early summers on a lake in Michigan, played high school football and took boxing lessons in a Chicago gym, where his nose was broken by a pro the first day. He ran away from home periodically, working as farm hand, dishwasher, sparring partner, and day laborer. Rejected for army service in 1914 because of a bad eye, he finally hitched to Kansas, lied about his age, and began writing obituaries for the *Kansas City Star*.

Hemingway never sought, as Milton exhorted, to make his life into a work of art—he was, rather, relentless in the determination to expose himself to the kind of experience of which art could be made. He quit Kansas City in the spring of 1917 and entered the war as a driver in the Norton-Harjes Ambulance Corps. Critically wounded in the leg on the Italian Front at Fossalta de Piave, he recuperated through the autumn of 1918 in a Milan hospital, where his nurse was an American Red Cross girl of Polish ancestry named Agnes von Kurowski.

Returning to Chicago shortly after his recovery, Hemingway met

[11] Cleanth Brooks, "Ernest Hemingway: Man on His Moral Uppers," *The Hidden God* (New Haven: Yale University Press, 1963), pp. 6–21.

[12] Jean-Paul Sartre, *Literary and Philosophical Essays* (New York: Criterion Books, Inc., 1955), pp. 34, 35, 38.

[13] John Killinger, *Hemingway and the Dead Gods* (Lexington: University of Kentucky Press, 1960).

Sherwood Anderson and married Hadley Richardson. In the winter of 1920, equipped with a letter of introduction from Anderson to Gertrude Stein, he returned to Paris as European correspondent for the *Toronto Star*. There, he eschewed the self-indulgent, histrionic sex, drink, and despair of his Lost Generation comrades, commandeered a table in the back of a St. Michel cafe, and practiced the hard, clear, disciplines of perception and expression in which Stein and Pound had instructed him. Their esthetic, in Hulme's phrase, courted "the exact curve of the thing," [14] or, as Hemingway himself later described it:

> . . . the greatest difficulty . . . was to put down what really happened in action; what the actual things were which produced the emotion which you experienced . . . the real thing, the sequence of motion and fact which made the emotion, and which would be valid in a year, or in ten years . . . or always.[15]

It was a technique of precise detail, ellipsis, and repetition. The signature was, finally, not a fumbling, lyric expressiveness which, innocent of irony, excluded the complexity of experience, but a tough, muted, inclusive distillation in the mode of drama.

> If a writer of prose knows enough about what he is writing about, he may omit things that he knows and the reader, if the writer is writing truly enough, will have a feeling of those things as strongly as though the writer had stated them. The dignity of movement of an iceberg is due to only one-eighth of it being above water. A writer who omits things because he does not know them only makes hollow places in his writing.[16]

Hemingway's early work in Paris consisted of a small volume, *Three Stories and Ten Poems*, followed in the spring of 1924 by *In Our Time*, a group of fierce and authentic vignettes of war and nature, including two reminiscences of his favorite matadors, Garcia and Villalta. His next volume was a *jeu d'esprit* parody of the later bathos of Sherwood Anderson, *Torrents of Spring*. *The Sun Also Rises*, published in 1926, was his first significant, extended piece of fiction, exploring not only the chaos of his fellow Wastelanders, wounded by the lethal abstractions of modern life, but the terms of possible regen-

---

[14] T. E. Hulme, "Romanticism and Classicism," *Speculations* (London, Routledge and Kegan Paul, Ltd., 1958).

[15] Ernest Hemingway, *Death in the Afternoon*, p. 2. For further discussion of Hemingway's principle, see T. S. Eliot's study of the "objective correlatve," "Hamlet and His Problems," *Selected Essays: 1917–32* (New York: Harcourt, Brace & World, Inc., 1932), pp. 124–25; and Eliseo Vivas, *Creation and Discovery* (New York: Noonday Press, Inc., 1955), p. 184.

[16] Hemingway, *Death in the Afternoon*, p. 192.

eration in the authentic life of the senses, the moral code of the bull-fighter. In 1929 he published *Men Without Women*, a volume of stories once more obsessed with his characteristic themes of war, nature, and the code.

Critics of *A Farewell to Arms* acknowledge unanimously the fine density of its texture, the power of its understatement, the toughness of its irony. Searching for its further significance, they have either extrapolated a variety of symbolic machineries, or denied that any exist. From the latter point of view, the novel is no more than a story of two lovers flattened by the obscenity of the war, their doom period-ically interrupted by a series of exercises in the acute rendering of the physical world, their philosophical peaks shining through a few clichés about burning ants, baseball, and getting "strong at the broken places."

We can, however, observe certain obsessive patterns in the novel's treatment of the love affair, the war, the natural world, and the fate that inscrutably directs, or fails to direct, it all. Hemingway's initial portraits of the surgeon and the priest suggest the book's preoccupa-tion with the drama of reasonable men caught up in the absurdity of a world at war. The surgeon practices his obsolete Sisyphian skill with stoic resignation—he is calm, still enjoys the pleasures of wine and prostitution, and even aspires toward a lost innocence in his comradeship with Henry and his solicitude for the first fumbling rituals of the love affair.

The priest's commitment is, in another way, more viciously refuted by the environment of war. If the surgeon's skill is disqualified by an operation that will never have time enough to heal, the priest's faith is undermined in the ruthless nihilism of the smoky cafes, where the only evidence of everlasting life is meaningless death. Yet he continues to defend his faith, exhorts Henry to go to the Abruzzi, "where the roads were frozen and hard as iron, where it was clear cold and dry and the snow was dry and powdery and hare-tracks in the snow . . . and there was good hunting" (p. 13), to undertake, perhaps, a mode of religious meditation which will clear his mind for the regeneration of his faith.

Henry himself, the narrator, lives in a house near the river, where there are "pebbles and boulders, dry and white in the sun, and the water was clear and swiftly moving and blue in the channels," a place where "the leaves fell early that year," and the road, after the soldiers, is "bare and white except for the leaves" (p. 3). The war continues, but in a world where "when the rains came the leaves all fell from the chestnut trees and the branches were bare and the trunks black with rain," "the vineyards were thin and bare-branched too and all

the country wet and brown and dead with the autumn," a world
where "small gray motor cars passed" that "splashed more mud than
the camions," and "if the car went especially fast it was the King"
(p. 4). It is as though he has already visited the "smoke of cafes,"
lived through the "nights when the room whirled and you needed to
look at the wall to make it stop . . ." (p. 13). For, later, the narrator
will explain how he became

> embarrassed by the words sacred, glorious, and sacrifice and the expres-
> sion in vain. We had heard them, sometimes standing in the rain almost
> out of earshot, so that only the shouted words came through, and had
> read them, on proclamations that were slapped up by billposters over
> other proclamations, now for a long time, and I had seen nothing sa-
> cred, and the things that were glorious had no glory and the sacrifices
> were like the stockyards at Chicago if nothing was done with the meat
> except to bury it. There were many words that you could not stand to
> hear and finally only the names of places had dignity. Certain numbers
> were the same way and certain dates and these with the names of places
> were all you could say and have them mean anything. Abstract words
> such as glory, honor, courage, or hallow were obscene beside the concrete
> names of villages, the numbers of regiments and the dates (p. 191).

These are the words which had driven him to the free fall of the
cafes and, eventually, to his staring at the wall, at the dense actuality
of his experience.

Henry watches the King pass by in a motor car and notices his
"little long-necked body and grey beard like a goat's chin tuft" (p. 5).
Waiting in a dugout, he gives each of his companions "a package of
cigarettes, Macedonias, loosely packed cigarettes that spilled tobacco
and needed to have the ends twisted before you smoked them" (p. 50).
Wounded in a minor skirmish, he is taken to a hospital where, await-
ing a visit from Rinaldi in the hot, fly-filled room, he observes that
the orderly "had cut paper into strips and tied the strips to a stick to
make a brush that swished the flies away" (p. 65). On the way to the
Milan hospital, sidetracked at Mestre, he becomes thirsty until someone "brought me a pulpy orange. I sucked on that and spit out the
pith . . ." (p. 81).

Once in the Milan hospital he soon becomes ambulatory, visits the
town with Catherine, where they "walked through the galleria . . .
stopped at the little place where they sold sandwiches; ham and let-
tuce sandwiches and anchovy sandwiches made of very tiny brown
glazed rolls and only about as long as your finger" (p. 117); and, on
another night, "drank a small bottle of chianti with the meal, had a
coffee afterward with a glass of cognac, finished the paper, put my
letters in my pocket, left the paper on the table with the tip and went
out" (p. 142).

Soon the famous Caporetto retreat begins, and Henry tells us how "in the night many peasants had joined the column from the roads of the country and in the column there were carts loaded with household goods; there were mirrors projecting up between mattresses, and chickens and ducks tied to carts. There was a sewing machine on the cart ahead of us in the rain. . . . On some carts the women sat huddled from the rain and others walked beside the carts keeping as close to them as they could. There were dogs now in the column, keeping under the wagons as they moved along. The road was muddy, the ditches at the side were high with water and beyond the trees that lined the road the fields looked too wet and too soggy to try to cross" (p. 205). In a little while he sees the Germans, two from the bicycle troops, ". . . ruddy and healthy looking. Their helmets came low down over their foreheads and the side of their faces. Their carbines were clipped to the frame of the bicycles. Stick bombs hung handle down from their belts. Their helmets and their grey uniforms were wet and they rode easily, looking ahead and to both sides" (p. 218). He stops at a barn to rest, hears the "rain on the roof and smelled the hay and, when I went down, the clean smell of dried dung in the stable" (p. 223).

Henry finally encounters a roadside kangaroo court where, dressed as he is in an Italian uniform, he expects to be shot as a German agitator. In a sudden impulse he "ducked down, pushed between two men, and ran for the river, my head down. I tripped at the edge and went in with a splash. The water was very cold and I stayed under as long as I could. I could feel the current swirl me and I stayed under until I thought I could never come up." He was lucky to find "a piece of timber" to hold on to, and he "lay in the icy water with my chin on the wood" until he approached the shore, where he could see "twigs on the willow bush" (p. 235). On the bank, he takes off his shoes, "emptied them of water," removes his coat, "took my wallet with my papers and my money all wet in it out of the inside pocket and then wrung the coat out," discovers, after he has slapped and rubbed and dressed again, that "I had lost my cap" (p. 236). Later he jumps a freight, bumps his head and slips in "under the canvas with guns. They smelled cleanly of oil and grease" as he "lay and listened to the rain on the canvas and the clicking of the car over the rails," looking at the guns with "their canvas jackets on." The bump on his head swollen, "lying still" to stop the bleeding, "letting it coagulate," he "picked away the dried blood except over the cut . . . feeling with my fingers I washed away where the dried blood had been, with rain-water that dripped from the canvas, and wiped it clean with the sleeve of my coat" (p. 239). He becomes "wet, cold and very hungry. . . . You did not love the floor of a flat-car nor guns with canvas jackets and the smell of vaselined metal or a canvas that rain leaked through, although it is very fine under a canvas and pleasant with guns" (p. 240).

In the days that follow, Henry rejoins Catherine, rows to Switzerland, and waits anxiously for the difficult resolution of her pregnancy, all the while visting wineshops that "smelled of early morning, of swept dust, spoons in coffee-glasses and the wet circles left by wineglasses," drinking "coffee . . . gray with milk," skimming the "milkscum off the top with a piece of bread" (p. 245). When they escape it is in a boat whose "oars were long and there were no leathers to keep them from slipping out," rowing slowly because he knew his "hands would blister" (p. 279). Looking back at an inn, he sees the "light coming from the windows and the woodcutters' horses stamping and jerking their heads outside to keep warm . . . frost on the hairs of their muzzles and their breathing made plumes of frost in the air" (p. 312).

In the final moments of Catherine's ordeal, Henry visits another cafe, "stood at the zinc bar and an old man served me a glass of white wine and a brioche. The brioche was yesterday's. I dipped it in the wine and then drank a glass of coffee." Outside, he notices the "refuse cans from the houses waiting for the collector," watches "a dog nosing at one of the cans" (p. 325). Still later, he has lunch, "a dish of sauerkraut with a slice of ham over the top and a sausage buried in the hot wine-soaked cabbage" (p. 328). A few minutes before the discovery of Catherine's fatal condition, he eats some ham and eggs "in a round dish—the ham underneath and the eggs on top . . . very hot and at the first mouthful I had to take a drink of beer to cool my mouth." He keeps drinking beer, notices, at last, the considerable "pile of saucers" now on his table, and the man "opposite . . . [who] had taken off his spectacles, put them away in a case, folded his paper and put it in his pocket and now sat holding his liqueur glass and looking out at the room" (p. 339). It is, finally, his cue to return to the hospital and the discovery of Catherine's death.

It is clear that the entire novel has registered Henry's sustained fixation on that wall, as though not merely the room but the meaning of life is whirling and only through such painstaking detail can anything human be salvaged.

Robert Penn Warren has remarked the implicit ladder of moral growth toward the code in Hemingway's fiction,[17] and we can trace the growth briefly in the three sections of *The Sun Also Rises*. There, the Hemingway hero suffers, first, the amoral chaos of the Paris cafes,

<hr>

[17] Warren, *Selected Essays*, pp. 80–118.

then seeks to purge himself in the authentic life of the senses on a fishing trip, and, finally, commits himself to a code of conduct born in the ruthless skill of Romero, the bullfighter. Later, the code is to be found in the familiar Hemingway world of boxer, big-game hunter, or soldier of fortune; in Harry Morgan, the simple patriarch, or Santiago, the enduring fisherman.

It is, then, as though *A Farewell to Arms* suffers the "Nada who art in Nada" of the smoky wartime cafes, respects the moral achievement in the surgeon's code, but prefers to focus on the second stage, the mode of authentic perception, furnishing its rationale in the priest's image of Abruzzi, and dramatizing its career in Henry's dogged determination to achieve direct sensory knowledge of the inexhaustible surfaces of the world. For, despite the routine cliché of its subject, there is nothing throughout the novel but the sense of felt life, experience with whose radical concreteness there can be no quarrel.

Henry, then, is the Hero as Esthetician, a modern man who is finished getting embarrassed in churches, exhausted by wine and dialectic, frustrated by the exclusiveness of fishing trips, walks in Abruzzi, and the literally unpracticeable disciplines of his abandoned architectural studies. In the ultimate chaos of his time, in a world at war, he is simply not impressed, and refuses to abbreviate his awareness of what it feels like to make love, ride in a freight car, or dive into a river. He will always insist on knowing what the weather is like. And, though in steady danger of boring us with the copiousness of his detail, Hemingway has provided his hero with irony sufficient to discourage the reader's impatience.

It is inevitable that Hemingway will pay equal attention to the sweetness of Henry's wine, the texture of the sheets under which he makes love, and the temperature of the water in which he escapes to his separate peace. For the big words, the meaningful hierarchies of civilized value, can no longer account for his experience. The important thing is to stop the room from whirling, and, for Hemingway's purposes, concentrating on a wall or a flower, the side of a mountain, or a package of cigarettes is equally valid.

Erich Auerbach, in discussing the representation of reality in contemporary Western literature, has remarked on the modern writer's obsession with the simple fact, the random occurrence:

What takes place . . . in works of this kind . . . is to put the emphasis on the random occurrence, to exploit it not in the service of a planned continuity of action but in itself, and in the process something new appears: nothing less than the wealth of reality and depth of life in every moment to which we surrender ourselves without prejudice. It is precisely the random moment which is comparatively independent of

the controversial and unstable orders over which men fight and despair;
it passes unaffected by them as daily life.

Auerbach, finally, is optimistic about the eventual recovery, through
this technique, of more sophisticated systems of value:

> The more it [the random occurrence] is exploited, the more the ele-
> mentary things which our lives have in common come to light. In this
> unprejudiced and exploratory type of representation we cannot but see
> to what extent—below the surface conflicts—the differences between
> men's way of life and forms of thought have already lessened. . . . It is
> still a long way to a common life of mankind on earth but the goal
> begins to be visible.[18]

There is, however, a further complexity in the structure of Hemingway's novel. For precisely as the chaos of war clears in tension against
the firm, precise, dense acts of perception, so the irony functions in
another way. It complicates, through the rich, suggestive, sensory
detail, the essentially pedestrian plot, the routine love story of wound,
hospital, separate peace, pregnancy, and death in childbirth. The style
of Henry's perception is employed as arbiter between the world's
unsubduable nightmare and the simple, tedious daylight of the personal life, focusing the war while expanding the love story.

It is, finally, on the basis of that love story, in its ostensible simplicity, in the supposed correlative superficiality of its protagonists,
that critics have habitually faulted the novel.

Wilhelm Worringer and, later, T. E. Hulme and Joseph Frank have
explored the modern writer's obvious preference for spatial over temporal form. In climates of relative cultural stability, the novel form
is habitually temporal, reflecting in the chronological progress of the
protagonist's life a development available through the moral and
religious order of his world, heightening the reader's "sense of active
participation in the organic." But where no order exists, where the
moment in time reflects only an eternal disorder, "a hundred visions
and revisions," the sense of everything happening at once, the writer
"reduces the appearances of the natural world to linear and geo-
metrical forms—forms which have the stability, the harmony, the sense
of order . . . [he] cannot find in the flux of phenomena." [19] As in
metaphor, experience is assembled as a series of atomistic surface con-
frontations—in *A Farewell to Arms* as a string of episodes in which
the lovers eat, drink, make love, visit the racetrack, and take walks

[18] Erich Auerbach, *Mimesis* (Princeton: Princeton University Press, 1953), p. 488.
[19] Wilhelm Worringer, *Abstraction and Empathy* (New York: International Uni-
versities Press, Inc., 1953); Hulme, *Speculations,* pp. 82–91; Joseph Frank, "Spatial
Form in Modern Literature: Part III," *Sewanee Review* 53 (1945): 643–53.

in the mountains. The partly repetitious, circular structure of William Faulkner's *Light in August* and Leopold Bloom's day in Dublin are more ambitiously developed examples of this style.

In Hemingway's love story, the fresh concrete surfaces of the fragmentary experiences renew the sense of life possible even in the cemetery of war, while, simultaneously, the lovers' instinct to develop their relationship from sex to love to, finally, an eagerness at the prospect of a child, reflects the persistent human effort not alone to make sense of life, but to believe it as well, to recover at last, in Auerbach's phrase, "the common life of mankind on earth."

Still, within the limits of the book's intention, a critic is justified in demanding that the characters make certain internal connections, not become fixated at the level of simple instruments sent out into battlefields, hospitals, and mountain cottages to register a plethora of sensory data.

Frederic Henry is a former student of architecture who has dropped out of his studies and volunteered as an ambulance driver. There is a certain gratuitousness about his presence in the war at all, but he has few illusions, is already bored with the monotonous routine of carnage and cafes, and feels more comfortable with road signs than with notions of sacrifice. He listens respectfully to the priest's recommendation of Abruzzi but knows that he will probably continue to visit the cafes, to reenact, in their sterility, the moral disaster of his time. Besides, there is always the chance that, once he gets to Abruzzi and clears his mind, he will have nothing to think about—always a danger in cults of sensation. Yet, in his initial courtship of Catherine, he is remarkably innocent, strangely capable of respecting qualities in a woman other than the simple weary skill of the prostitute.

It will be useful, at this point, to explore more fully the ostensible insufficiency of the Hemingway style to treat a complicated human experience, the experience, for example, of the initial lovemaking in the hospital. If an author wishes to set the affair in a hospital, he would seem obliged to acknowledge the hospital's shadow on the scene, its gloss on the affair as somehow mortally wounded. But Hemingway locks it at the level of prank, complete with bedpans and wine bottles, rising temperature charts and careless prophylaxis. The irony, unacknowledged, would appear to dismiss their coitus as simply another set of defective twitches between antiseptic sheets, or, humorously, as some form of *ultimate* therapy.

Yet, even here, the cynicism will not work. The unacknowledged irony would effectively demolish the scene if it were allowed to remain at the level of cliché, if the lovers were too aware of their environment and turned the affair into an embarrassing, willed engagement

of superhuman sexual endurance, or simply ignored it and acted out
its own haunting paralysis. Hemingway's solution has been to have
them accept the hospital as simply the place where their love affair
has to begin, the narrator taking the context as seriously as he takes
the rest of his experience, pausing to notice a bat flying into the room
who "was not frightened but hunted in the room as though he had
been outside." In the morning, "we smelled the dew on the roofs and
then the coffee of the men at the gun on the next roof" (p. 106). The
cliche, in short, is revivified in a rich, suggestive, completely human
texture.

The underground opera of Henry's desertion appears to constitute
another failure to exploit, as Richards has said, the meanings latent
in the context—an effort to generate more emotion than the experience warrants.[20] The critic has no qualms about Henry going AWOL,
only about what he is expected to make of it—a "separate peace,"
some form of cleansed rebirth? He would insist that the book indicate to us that it knows that Henry's impulsive defection is nothing
more—certainly not a solemn act of abjuration.

But the rationale of Henry's escape is far simpler:

> You had lost your cars and your men as a floorwalker loses the stock
> of his department in a fire. . . . You were out of it now. You had no
> more obligation. If they shot floorwalkers after a fire in the department
> store because they spoke with an accent they had always had, then cer-
> tainly the floorwalkers would not be expected to return when the store
> opened again for business (p. 241).

Henry, again, avoids both extremes, refusing either to run amok in
some absurd demonstration against violence, or to withdraw into a
highbrow shell shock, the ultimate version of the sterile dialectic of
the smoky cafes. He simply does all he can do, noticing, with painstaking sanity, that "I was not made to think. I was made to eat. My
God, yes. Eat and drink and sleep with Catherine. Tonight maybe . . .
a good meal and sheets and never going away again except together.
. . . I lay and thought where we would go. There were many places"
(p. 242).

When he emerges from the Tagliamento and makes his "separate
peace," it is simply a quiet, private gesture in behalf of life, a reenact-
ment of his earlier impatience with the big words "sacred, glorious,
and sacrifice and the expression in vain." For the "big words" on the
Caporetto retreat have come, finally, to mean suicide, and the pact is
a partly self-dramatic, but eminently sane letter of resignation. Only
a madman could call it a betrayal.

[20] I. A. Richards, *Philosophy of Rhetoric* (Oxford: Oxford University Press, 1936),
p. 55.

Catherine Barkley has a waif-like, lover-*cum*-partner identity at the beginning. She seems glorified by all those characteristics that the insecure, boyish lover Hemingway has been called would idealize in a woman—she is easy but, somehow, irrevocably pure; has the strength of Beowulf, yet falls apart in a hotel room at the reflection that she is behaving like a whore; is gentle as a deer, and still, in the boat on the way to Switzerland, muses rather crudely about the advantages of being poked "in the tummy" by Henry's oar.

The crucial demurrer about Catherine, however, is her pregnancy. The book arranges for nothing more than an accident, and we might, after all, accept it that way. Though she is a nurse, we know that even nurses get careless in the swirl of such passion. But the logical response, without a ring and surrounded by the vicissitudes of war, should have been abortion, for she even confesses that she has tried everything else. Though she sentimentally presses a St. Anthony medal on Henry at one point, it is clear that she has no religion which would have made that operation intolerable.

Though Catherine is, admittedly, a pleasant, tough little companion, a version of the woman as partner, it is obvious that if she lacked such courage and resource she could hardly have survived at all in a world at war. She is, however, feminine enough on her first night with Henry in the hotel room to feel ashamed, somehow derelict, a tramp. Still, the reader suspects the efficient, businesslike detachment with which she rigs her schedule at the hospital to enable the sex with Henry. Yet again, the very fact of her pregnancy guarantees, in its careless abandon, the sincere intensity of the love affair. Further, though she continually whines about seeing Henry dead in the rain, and though she naïvely makes her token bet at the racetrack, she can also, during the boat trip, resent her unpropitious maternity. She is, finally, a girl who, at the point of death, pleads with Henry not to "do our things with another girl, or say the same things . . ." (p. 342). Her complexity crystallizes at last, for the woman she is yearns for the reassurance, yet only the frank, open, tough little partner would have the audacity to demand it. She has, then, all along particularized the daily experiences of her life. In the final hours before death she seems to achieve a similar, more memorable concreteness for her identity as well.

In Hemingway's final irony, she is destroyed, not by the war, but by the small hips that would have killed her in Minneapolis, by the same inscrutable fate that arranges for retreats at Caporetto, lovemaking in Milan, and, ultimately, the perennial resource of Abruzzi.

Hemingway's solution throughout *A Farewell to Arms* has been neither to succumb to the war's paralyzing morbidity nor to undertake to resist directly its violent catastrophe. It has been, rather, to focus on what is immediate and dense, and unequivocal and human in the narrator's experience of it. The novel's achievement is in its determination to exploit, if sometimes too painstakingly, the ground on which, if it is ever possible again, a meaningful vision of the human condition will have to be constructed. The style, in short, has been made the symbol.

PART ONE

Interpretations

The Unadulterated Sensibility

by Ray B. West, Jr.

I

Ernest Hemingway's first three important works were *In Our Time,* a collection of curiously related short stories; *The Sun Also Rises,* his first serious and successful novel; and *A Farewell to Arms.* All three deal with the same subject: the condition of man in a society upset by the violence of war. The short stories, while complete (almost idyllic) within themselves, take on an added dimension when viewed against the animal-cruelty of the connecting war scenes. *The Sun Also Rises,* although set in the postwar period, is conditioned by the wartime disability of its principal figure, Jake Barnes. But the setting for *A Farewell to Arms* is the war itself, and the romance of Frederic Henry and Catherine Barkley, their attempt to escape the war and its resulting chaos, is a parable of twentieth-century man's disgust and disillusionment at the failure of civilization to achieve the ideals it had been promising throughout the nineteenth century. While the relation of one story to another in *In Our Time* is more or less arbitrary, while the meandering action of the ex-patriots' excursion into Spain in *The Sun Also Rises* is at most emblematic, the sequence of events in *A Farewell to Arms* is ordered and logical to an extreme which (outside of Henry James) is the exception in the American novel.

As a matter of fact, the physical form of *A Farewell to Arms* more nearly resembles the drama than it does the majority of American works of fiction. It is composed of five separate books, each composed of a series of scenes, and each scene broken into sections which might be likened to stage direction and dialogue. Thus, in section one we

"The Unadulterated Sensibility" (original title: *"Ernest Hemingway:* A Farewell to Arms"). *From* The Art of Modern Fiction *by Ray B. West, Jr. (New York: Holt, Rinehart & Winston, Inc., 1949), pp. 139–51. Copyright © 1949 by Holt, Rinehart & Winston, Inc. First published in* The Sewanee Review 55 *(Winter 1945):* 120–35. *Reprinted by permission of Holt, Rinehart & Winston, Inc., and* The Sewanee Review.

have the introduction of all major characters, the general war setting, and a statement of the problems involved; in section two the development of the romance between Frederic and Catherine; in section three, the retreat at Caporetto and the decision of Frederic to escape the chaos of war; in section four, the supposed escape, the rowing of Frederic and Catherine across the lake into Switzerland; and in section five, the hope of sanctuary which, through a reversal reminiscent again of the drama, comes to a climax in the ironic scene of Catherine's death while giving birth to their child.

As Robert Penn Warren has pointed out (*Kenyon Review*: Winter, 1947), *A Farewell to Arms,* while not a religious book in the usual sense, depends upon a consciousness of the religious problems of our time. Its subject is the search for truth—for ethical standards to replace those which seemed impossible under the wartime conditions which it depicts. The use of the Christian religion is not, however, confined to the conventional uses of the ordinary religious novel, in which the characters are evaluated according to their acceptance or rejection of orthodox views. Rather, it is ironically implied, for instance, that Catherine, who is repeatedly portrayed as one with no orthodox religious sense, is really on the side of the priest, whose orthodoxy is beyond question. It is implied, too, that the priest's religious sensibility, like the sensibility of all of the participants in the novel's action, is heightened by the events of the war. After the difficult summer, during which Frederic was confined in the hospital, all of the men in his group have been softened. "Where are all the good old priest-baiters?" Rinaldi asks. "Do I have to bait this priest alone without support?" Frederic could see that the baiting which had gone on earlier did not touch the priest now. In talking with the priest he makes a distinction which is important to our interpretation of all the characters: even the priest is now not only technically a Christian, he is more like Our Lord. "It is," Frederic says, "in defeat that we become Christians."

On the other hand, it is not merely the humility of defeat, but the result of active participation (a firsthand acquaintance with the objective facts instead of the abstract theories of warfare) which makes all the difference. Outward forms divorced from action do not suffice, as when the soldier under Frederic refuses to believe that the Austrians were going to attack, because, as he said, "What has been done this summer cannot have been done in vain." Frederic thinks:

> I was always embarrassed by the words sacred, glorious, and sacrifice and the expression in vain. We had heard them, sometimes standing in the rain almost out of earshot, so that only the shouted words came through, and had read them, on proclamations that were slapped up by billposters over other proclamations, now for a long time, and I had seen nothing

sacred, and the things that were glorious had no glory and the sacrifices were like the stockyards at Chicago if nothing was done with the meat except to bury it. There were many words that you could not stand to hear and finally only the names of places had dignity.

When the words became separated from the acts they were meant to describe, then they meant nothing; the slaughter of war was less than the slaughter of animals in the stockyard. The names of places had dignity because the places still had some objective reality. Likewise, the acts of Rinaldi when he is practicing his craft, of Dr. Valentini (but not of the incompetent physicians), have dignity because they are done surely and skillfully—to some purpose. The early stages of Frederic and Catherine's courtship were like moves in a chess game or a game of bridge; later it became something different, so different that even the outward form of marriage could make no difference. Catherine asks: "What good would it do to marry now? We're really married. I couldn't be any more married." Even the war, when Frederic was no longer participating, "seemed as far away as the football games of some one else's college." No activity has meaning unless the participant is emotionally involved; this is the real test, like the names of places. There is Christianity and there are true Christians. There is incompetence and competence. There is marriage and there is true love. In a story in *In Our Time,* we have the picture of a bullfighter who is defeated and derided by the crowd, but he is really "The Undefeated" (the title of the story), because he is only outwardly not inwardly defeated. As we have seen, in "The Short Happy Life" even death does not defeat Francis Macomber, for it is in death that he triumphs.

But what is the real distinction between the failures—the defeated —and the *genuine* men and women in the novel—what critics have come to call "the initiated"? Rinaldi (who is one of them) says to Frederic at the time when Frederic returns to the front: "You puncture me when I become a great Italian thinker. But I know many things I can't say." Frederic, when he is talking to the priest after his return from the hospital, says: "I never think and yet when I begin to talk I say the things I have found out in my mind without thinking." There are times when Catherine "feels" immoral, but most of the time she "feels" that her love is sanctified. The peasants and the defeated soldiers have wisdom because they are not misled by the empty forms. Hemingway seems to be saying, like William Wordsworth, that such men are by circumstance closer to reality—and thus to wisdom. In the book which followed *A Farewell to Arms*—*Death in the Afternoon*—Hemingway says, "Morals are what you feel good after." Brett Ashley in *The Sun Also Rises* decides to give up a love affair because it makes her *feel* good "deciding not to be a bitch."

The test of morals is the unadulterated sensibility—the sensibility not misled by the empty forms of patriotism, religion, and love: the sensibility of Rinaldi when he does not attempt to be a great Italian thinker; the sensibility of Dr. Valentini, who knows at once what is to be done and does it without quibble and consultation; the sensibility of the peasants; the sensibility of Catherine, who learns from her love for Frederic that it is all right, who says: "Everything we do seems so innocent and simple. I can't believe we do anything wrong." Even the sensibility of Frederic, which is the developing moral sense of the novel, is superior to Rinaldi's because it has greater scope—the surgeon is happy only when he is working. "I know more than you," Rinaldi says, and Frederic agrees with him. "But you will have a better time. Even with remorse you will have a better time."

It is this limiting quality in Frederic's character which points to the principal problem of the novel. Rinaldi calls it remorse. Frederic cannot completely escape the forms of his early training, though he makes a systematic progress throughout the book. Before he was wounded he had attempted to accept Catherine's philosophy that death is the end, but his experience seemed to prove otherwise, for in her antireligious position Catherine is as orthodox as the priest. Frederic says: "I felt myself rush bodily out of myself and out and out and out and all the time bodily in the wind. I went out swiftly, all of myself, and I knew I was dead and that it had all been a mistake to think you just died." This is Hemingway's mysticism which triumphed in *For Whom the Bell Tolls* and which was at its lowest ebb in his curious little essay "A Natural History of the Dead." Frederic does not love God, but he is afraid of him in the night sometimes. Because he does not "belong," he and Catherine cannot find sanctuary in the church the evening they are waiting for the train, though an Italian couple does. Yet Frederic is much more anxious about the absence of the marriage ceremony than Catherine, and when the child is born dead he is disturbed because it had not been baptized. The limitations of Frederic's religious sensibility (a symbol for the religious sensibility of our time) are depicted in two scenes, the first in his failure to visit the home of the priest at Abruzzi, where "You would like the people and though it is cold it is clear and dry"; the second is the incident at the church:

> There were streetcar tracks and beyond them was the cathedral. It was white and wet in the mist. We crossed the tram tracks. On our left were the shops, their windows lighted, and the entrance to the galleria. There was a fog in the square and when we came close to the front of the cathedral it was very big and the stone was wet.
> "Would you like to go in?"
> "No," Catherine said. We walked along. There was a soldier standing with his girl in the shadow of one of the stone buttresses ahead of us and

we passed them. They were standing tight up against the stone and he had put his cape around her.

"They're like us," I said.

"Nobody is like us," Catherine said. She did not mean it happily.

"I wish they had some place to go."

"It mightn't do them any good."

"I don't know. Everybody ought to have some place to go."

"They have the cathedral," Catherine said. (XXIII, 157)

Catherine and Frederic have a hotel room (the "lost generation"), while the Italian soldier and his girl have the cathedral; the priest has his cold, clear, dry country; the atheists have their houses of prostitution. The priest's country appeals to Frederic, and he is sorry he did not visit it while he was on leave:

> I had wanted to go to Abruzzi. I had gone to no place where the roads were frozen and hard as iron, where it was clear cold and dry and the snow was dry and powdery and hare-tracks in the snow and the peasants took off their hats and called you Lord and there was good hunting. I had gone to no such place but to the smoke of cafés and nights when the room whirled and you needed to look at the wall to make it stop, nights in bed, drunk, when you know that that was all there was, and the strange excitement of waking and not knowing who it was with you, and the world all unreal in the dark and so exciting that you must resume again unknowing and not caring in the night, sure that this was all and all and all and not caring. (III, 13)

Here is the symbol of Frederic's predicament, a key passage, since it represents the religious contrast. The priest's religion is his clear, cold country; Catherine's religion is her love, which, as Count Greffi says, "is a religious feeling," or, as Catherine tells Frederic: "You're my religion. You're all I've got." Frederic is the modern hero, lost between two worlds, the world of tradition and certainty which he cannot wholly relinquish, and the exciting but uncertain world of the twentieth century, where you only occasionally find something substantial to look at to make everything stop whirling, where you live for the moment, giving yourself up to sensations, for it is through the senses that you discover truth: the strong man giving equal odds to his weaker opponent, the boxer, the hunter, the bullfighter, the soldier, and the lover; the strong man aware that the only order in the universe is that which he himself can supply, but aware, too, that such order is transitory, that perhaps the highest possible values consist in pure sensation which seeks out new order and a stoicism which transcends physical defeat.

II

At the beginning Frederic wavers between reason and sensibility, between formal religion and "true" Christianity, between the empty forms of love and true love. He has been thrust into a world of violent action in which choice is eventually to become necessary. An English critic has called Frederic "a curiously passive hero," but this is true only in the sense that Thomas Mann's Herr Friedemann was passive. The Hemingway hero is, theoretically, passive, because he is allied to nature through his unreason, but his particular dilemma usually has all the appearances of active seeking.

Frederic's relationship to Catherine in Book I is like a game of bridge where you pretend to be playing for stakes, but do not know what the stakes are. At the end of the section Frederic is wounded, but not seriously. It is the first hint that what he had called "the picturesque front" was capable of becoming something else. It is a foreshadowing of the retreat at Caporetto.

In Book II the action takes place in the American hospital at Milan, and almost at once we know that the formal relationship (love like a bridge game or a game of chess) has ended. Frederic thinks:

> God knows I had not wanted to fall in love with her. I had not wanted to fall in love with any one. But God knows I had and I lay on the bed in the room of the hospital in Milan and all sorts of things went through my head but I felt wonderful . . . (XIV, 100)

We are introduced to the incompetent doctors and to the professional patriots like Ettore. Frederic, although he cannot reject Ettore as completely as Catherine, does reject his own decoration, because he knows that he is not a hero. The silver medal repeats the pattern of the empty form. A new action is suggested in this book by Catherine's fear of death. She is afraid of the rain, she says, and when pressed by Frederic for an explanation, admits that it is because she sometimes sees herself dead in it. Frederic is unbelieving. "And sometimes I see you dead in it," she adds. "That's more likely," Frederic says. "No it's not, darling. Because I can keep you safe. I know I can. But nobody can help themselves." Here is one of the secrets of the passivity of Hemingway's characters. Later in the section, when Catherine admits that she is going to have a baby:

> "You aren't angry are you, darling?"
> "No."
> "And you don't feel trapped?"
> "Maybe a little. But not by you."

"I didn't mean by me. You must be stupid. I meant trapped at all."
"You aways feel trapped biologically." (XXI, 148)

"Biologically," in the Hemingway world, covers just about everything; there is nothing you can do about life but accept it with stoicism. This is an anticipation of the final scenes in the novel, but Frederic, fortunately, did not realize how final the trap was:

> Poor, poor dear Cat. And this was the price you paid for sleeping together. This was the end of the trap. This was what people got for loving each other. (XLI, 341–42)

In this book, however, the threat is taken only seriously enough to provoke discussion of death and the conditions of man's dying. Frederic has quoted the line, "The coward dies a thousand deaths, the brave but one"; Catherine replies: "The brave dies perhaps two thousand deaths if he's intelligent. He simply doesn't mention them."

There is an indication that Frederic is very little different from Catherine in his fear of death. They are in a café and it is raining. He quotes Andrew Marvell: "But at my back I always hear/Time's wingéd chariot hurrying near." He wants to talk facts. Where will the baby be born? Catherine refuses stoically) to discuss it. "Then don't worry, darling," she tells him. "You were fine until now and now you're worrying."

The tone of this section suggests death, but the reader does not know, any more than do Catherine and Frederic, whose death it is to be. Frederic returns to the front, where there are rumors of a new attack by the Austrians. Catherine awaits the time when she will have her baby. Both are, in a sense, trapped—trapped by the war, by their love, and (though they are unaware of it) by death.

At the very beginning of Book III we are introduced to the town of Caporetto. Frederic "remembered it as a little white town with a campanile in a valley. It was a clean little town and there was a fine fountain in the square." This is where the summer fighting has ended. One of Hemingway's most constant symbols of the goal which his heroes seek is—to ultilize the title of one of his stories—a "Clean, Well-Lighted Place." War has undoubtedly destroyed the "clean little town," but this is just an additional indication of war's ugliness. Caporetto is the point where the Austrians succeed in breaking through and turning Frederic's "picturesque front" into a machine of destruction. There are only isolated examples of decency and order in the retreat; the whole atmosphere is one of anarchy and confusion.

Malcolm Cowley has likened Frederic's plunge into the river to escape execution as a baptism—a symbol of Frederic's entering the world of the initiated, but this is true only in so far as it refers to his decision (his rebirth) concerning the war. The chapters preceding, where Frederic returns to the front and meets his old comrades, indicate both how much he had learned through his stay at the hospital (the baptism of love) and how much the members of his company have learned through the difficult fighting of the summer (their baptism of fire), but the final consecration does not come until later when Frederic is confronted by love and death at the same time. The retreat does, however, represent a major phase in his initiation. Frederic is in the position of the fat gray-haired little lieutenant-colonel whom the carabinieri were questioning at the bridge.

> The questioners had all the efficiency, coldness and command of themselves of Italians who are firing and are not being fired on.
> "Your brigade?"
> He told them.
> "Regiment?"
> He told them.
> "Why are you not with your regiment?"
> He told them.
> "Do you not know that an officer should be with his troops?"
> He did.
> That was all. Another officer spoke.
> "It is you and such as you that have let the barbarians onto the sacred soil of the fatherland."
> "I beg your pardon," said the lieutenant-colonel.
> "It is because of treachery such as yours that we have lost the fruits of victory."
> "Have you ever been in a retreat?" the lieutenant-colonel asked.
> (XXX, 239)

The military police are firing but are not being fired on. They are like religious persons who have never been tempted, condemning the sinner who has succumbed; the police have the hollow shell of patriotism, using such phrases as "the sacred soil of the fatherland" and "the fruits of victory," but it is punctured by the lieutenant-colonel's simple question: "Have you ever been in a retreat?" The carabiniere's brave words have no relation to the reality of the situation, while the condemned man's question goes right to the heart of it. Frederic rationalizes his own situation as follows:

> You had lost your cars and your men as a floorwalker loses the stock of his department in a fire. There was, however, no insurance. You were out of it now. You had no more obligation. If they shot the floorwalker after a fire in the department store because they spoke with an accent they had always had, then certainly the floorwalkers would not be expected to return when the store opened again for business. They might seek other employment; if there was any other employment and the police did not get them.
> Anger was washed away in the river along with any obligation. Al-

though that ceased when the carabiniere put his hands on my collar. I would like to have had the uniform off *although I did not care much about the outward forms* [our italics] I had taken off the stars, but that was for convenience. It was no point of honor. I was not against them. I was through. I wished them all the luck. There were the good ones, and the brave ones, and the calm ones, and the sensible ones, and they deserved it. But it was not my show any more and I wished this bloody train would get to Mestre and I would eat and stop thinking. I would have to stop. (XXXII, 248)

The fighter obeys the rules until they are suspended or no longer enforced; then he gets out of the ring (cf. Margot Macomber in "The Short Happy Life"). With the retreat at Caporetto, the Austrian front ceased to be "the picturesque front"; it is no longer subject to the traditional rules of "honorable" warfare. Frederic, too, for the time being ceases to be the "curiously passive hero." He cannot escape the war until he escapes from Italy with Catherine, and to escape is to struggle.

Yet according to the standards of Frederic Henry's world, such a decision is in itself dangerous. His reasoning is too pat, his assurance too great. The determination to struggle becomes a kind of "tragic flaw"—a brash modern pride which tempts fate as the occupants of Stephen Crane's little boat tempt the seven mad gods of the sea. Hemingway hints at this in the beginning of Book IV. In the hotel at Stresa, where Frederic went to find Catherine, the barman asks him questions about the war.

"Don't talk about the war," I said. The war was a long way off. Maybe there wasn't any war. There was no war here. Then I realized it was over for me. But I did not have the feeling that it was really over. I had the feeling of a boy who thinks of what is happening at a certain hour at the schoolhouse from which he has played truant. (XXXIV, 262)

The war is not over. Even after the successful effort to leave Italy and enter Switzerland, the war (which is really a symbol for the chaos of nature—the biological trap) catches up with Frederic and Catherine. It is significant that Frederic's reason tells him he can escape—that he *has* escaped; his sensibility suggests that he is only playing truant. Frederic felt like a masquerader in his civilian clothes. That is to say, in the modern sense, all happiness is a form of truancy. The months in Switzerland were idyllic. Even the snow came late, almost as though Frederic had ordered nature's cooperation.

The trap is sprung in Book V. Catherine's confinement is difficult, and the birth when it does come is finally performed through a Caesarean operation. The child is born dead. Catherine herself dies soon afterward. Yet, though it is Catherine who dies, *A Farewell to Arms* is not her tragedy. Unlike Francis Macomber and unlike Manuelo in "The Undefeated," she does not *become* admirable in her dying; she *remains* admirable according to the rules of decorum which Hemingway has set up:

> The nurse opened the door and motioned with her finger for me to come. I followed her into the room. Catherine did not look up when I came in. I went over to the side of the bed. The doctor was standing by the bed on the opposite side. Catherine looked at me and smiled. I bent down over the bed and started to cry.
> "Poor darling," Catherine said very softly. She looked gray.
> "You're all right, Cat," I said. "You're going to be all right."
> "I'm going to die," she said; then waited and said, "I hate it."
> I took her hand.
> "Don't touch me," she said. I let go of her hand. She smiled. "Poor darling. You touch me all you want."
> "You'll be all right, Cat. I know you'll be all right."
> "I meant to write you a letter to have if anything happened, but I didn't do it."
> "Do you want me to get a priest or any one to come and see you?"
> "Just you," she said. Then a little later, "I'm not afraid. I just hate it."
> (XLI, 353–54)

Catherine had had the perception of death early, but it had come to Frederic only since learning of the doctor's fears. During the operation he thought she was dead: "Her face was gray." Catherine knows intuitively that she is going to die. Frederic senses it, but his reason will not allow him to accept it, as she does, as "just a dirty trick."

> I knew she was going to die and I prayed that she would not. Don't let her die. Oh, God, please don't let her die. I'll do anything for you if you won't let her die. Please, please, please, dear God, don't let her die. Dear God, don't let her die. Please, please, please don't let her die. God please make her not die. I'll do anything you say if you don't let her die. You took the baby but don't let her die. That was all right, but don't let her die. Please, please, dear God, don't let her die. (XLI, 353)

Frederic's hope that he could prevent her from dying is as illusory as his belief that he could escape the war by signing a separate peace. In a sense, Frederic is a depiction of the narrator's figure in "The Open Boat," who, when he realizes that there is no tangible thing to hoot, feels the desire to confront a personification and indulge in pleas. It isn't until he has accepted the terrible reality of Catherine's death that he is truly initiated: "It was like saying good-by to a statue." This is the biological trap—sprung. Catherine has been right from the beginning. Early in the novel, in speaking of her English lover who was killed in France, she says: "I thought perhaps he couldn't stand it and then of course he was killed and that was the end of it." "I don't know," Frederic said. "Oh, yes," Catherine emphasizes. "That's the end of it."

These are the limits, then, as circumscribed by nature: death is the end of life. After death there is only the lifeless statue. It was this conclusion (or something like it) which caused Gertrude Stein to say of Ernest Hemingway that he belonged to the "lost generation," lost because the comfortable morality of the nineteenth century had been denied them after 1914. Frederic Henry attempts to believe in the validity of warfare, but even the peasant soldiers under him know better. When he puts his trust in religion or in his love for Catherine he is also defeated. He reasons it out as follows:

> That was what you did. You died. You did not know what it was about. You never had time to learn. They threw you in and told you the rules and the first time they caught you off base they killed you. (XLI, 350)

In "The Short Happy Life of Francis Macomber" the emphasis was upon man's final victory over death. That view is represented here in the stoical death of Catherine, but the emphasis is upon futility. In a striking image which represents the key scene in the novel, we have Frederic thinking about an experience he has had:

> Once in camp I put a log on top of the fire and it was full of ants. As it commenced to burn, the ants swarmed out and went first toward the centre where the fire was; then turned back and ran toward the end. When there were enough on the end they fell off into the fire. Some got out, their bodies burnt and flattened, and went off not knowing where they were going. But most of them went toward the fire and back toward the end and swarmed on the cool end and finally fell off into the fire. I remember thinking at the time that it was the end of the world and a splendid chance to be a messiah and lift the log off the fire and throw it out where the ants could get off onto the ground. But I did not do anything but throw a tin cup of water on the log, so that I would have the cup empty to put whiskey in before I added water to it. I think the cup of water on the burning log only steamed the ants. (XLI, 350)

The relationship of this parable to Catherine's predicament is unmistakable. For her there is likewise no messiah to come to the rescue. Death is the end of it, and the only value in death is man's knowledge of it. In Ernest Hemingway's novels, those who live well die like heroes. They are the initiated. But the initiation of Frederic Henry comes gradually. He learns about war, love, and finally death. Catherine's death is the final stage in his initiation.

III

If this conclusion is true, we might ask: "Why the title: *A Farewell to Arms*"? The title suggests in its obvious implications that the author saw his subject concerned primarily with the war. In that case, we might say either that we are wrong in our conclusions or that the author was wrong in his selection of title. This raises the question of Ernest Hemingway's method—his style. Hemingway's sensibility, when it is functioning at its highest point, has always worked upon an immediate objective level which translates ideas into terms of concrete things: life as a baseball game where each error is punished by death or compared to the struggle of ants on a burning log, the comparison of a hero's death with the slaughter of animals at a stockyard. In each case we are aware of the double implication, the idea and the image; and the emotional force of the idea is intensified by the shock supplied by the image. This is the more complicated form of Hemingway's noted "understatement." At the time of Catherine's operation, while the doctor has gone to make his preparations, Frederic is left to administer the anesthesia. He has been told that the correct amount would register upon the dial at number 2, but when Catherine is in extreme pain, he says, "I turned the dial to three and then four. I wished the doctor would come back. I was afraid of the numbers above two." The statement "I wished the doctor would come back" is understatement. The use of the machine–image suggests Catherine's immediate danger. Another author might have examined in great detail both Catherine's illness and the emotion which Frederic was experiencing at that time; but from the simple, quiet statement, reinforced by the dial registering the numbers above two, we get the full force of Frederic's terror in a few strokes.

That Hemingway was aware of this quality is evidenced by the statement which he once made that what he was attempting to get was a "fifth dimension" in his prose; not the ordinary dimensions of exposition and description, but the full quality of the emotional experience. This is not an unusual characteristic of a work of art; it is merely Ernest Hemingway's means of explaining his own intention; but it suggests the caution a reader should exercise in taking the author's words or sentences at their most obvious level of meaning. Perhaps this is true also of the title, *A Farewell to Arms*. Someone has suggested somewhere that the "Arms" referred not to the war, but to the arms of Catherine; thus suggesting that what the novel was about, really, was Frederic's loss of his love. This is as limited an interpretation as that which sees the novel as only a "war novel."

A more valid interpretation would see the title as completely ironic. Frederic has attempted to escape from the obligations which life imposes. He did not wish to fall in love, but he did. He attempted to escape the war, but he felt like a schoolboy who was playing truant. His life with Catherine in Switzerland and the life which they anticipated after the war were relatively devoid of conflict. Catherine and Frederic had said farewell to the life of action and struggle, but ironically their greatest test—the attempt to save the life of Catherine—came at the very moment when they seemed to have achieved a successful escape.

What the novel says, finally, is that you cannot escape the obligations of action—you cannot say "farewell to arms"; you cannot sign a separate peace. You can only learn to live with life, to tolerate it as "the initiated" learn to tolerate it.

Loser Take Nothing

by Philip Young

A Farewell to Arms (1929) which borrows its title from a poem of that name by George Peele,[1] reverts to the war and supplies background for *The Sun Also Rises*. For the germs of both of its plots, a war plot and a love plot, it reaches back to *In Our Time*. An outline of the human arms in the novel is to be found among these early stories in a piece called "A Very Short Story." This sketch, less than two pages long, dealt quickly, as the novel does extensively, with the drinking and love-making in an Italian hospital of an American soldier, wounded in the leg, and a nurse, and had told of their love and their wish to get married. But where the book ends powerfully with the death in childbirth of the woman, the story dribbled off in irony. The lovers parted, the soldier leaving for home to get a job so that he could send for his sweetheart. Before long, however, the nurse wrote that she had a new lover who was going to marry her, though he never did; and then, shortly after receiving the letter, the soldier "contracted gonorrhea from a sales girl in a loop department store while riding in a taxicab through Lincoln Park."[2]

The war plot of *A Farewell to Arms*, on the other hand, is a greatly expanded version of that Chapter VI sketch in which Nick was wounded and made his separate peace—with Rinaldi, who also appears in the longer work. This wound, which got Nick in the spine, and

---

"Loser Take Nothing" (Editor's title). From Ernest Hemingway: A Reconsideration *by Philip Young (University Park: Pennsylvanian State University Press, 1966), pp. 89–95. Copyright © 1966 by Philip Young. Reprinted by permission of the author.*

[1] As in the case of many of Hemingway's titles, the allusion to the poem is slightly ironic, for Peele mourned the fact that he could no longer fight.

[2] Except for the venereal element (which according to a paperback biographer was thus contracted by a *friend* of the author), it appears that this sketch tells how it actually was, the novel-to-be how it might have been. In life Catherine Barkley, the heroine of the novel, was Agnes H. von Kurowski, the Bellevue-trained daughter of a German-American father; Hemingway intended to bring her home from Italy and marry her. (Leicester's biography prints an excellent photograph of her; Marcelline's biography prints a picture Ernest sent home from Italy of a "nice-looking bearded older man . . . Count Greppie"—possibly the model for Count Greffi in the novel.)

"I" in the knee, and emasculated Jake, has returned to the knee,
which is where Hemingway was most badly hit. Then the same story
is rehearsed again in lengthened form. Recuperated enough to return
to action after another convalescence in Milan, Lt. Frederic Henry becomes bitter about the society responsible for the war and, caught up in
the Italian retreat from Caporetto, he breaks utterly with the army
in which he is an officer. And this is again the old protagonist, who
cannot sleep at night for thinking—who must not use his head to
think with, and will absolutely have to stop it. He is also the man
who, when he does sleep, has nightmares, and wakes from them in
sweat and fright, and goes back to sleep in an effort to stay outside
his dreams.

Unlike Jake Barnes, however, Frederic Henry participates fully in
the book's action, and as a person is wholly real. But he is also a
little more than that, for just as the response of Americans of the
period to the aimless and disillusioned hedonism of Jake and his
friends indicated that some subtle chord in them had been struck,
so something in the evolution of Frederic Henry from complicity in
the war to bitterness and escape has made him seem, though always
himself, a little larger than that, too. Complicity, bitterness, escape—
a whole country could read its experience, Wilson to Harding, in his,
and it began to become clear that in Hemingway as elsewhere "hero"
meant not simply "protagonist" but a man who stands for many men.
Thus it is that when historians of various kinds epitomize the temper
of the American Twenties and a reason for it the adventures of that
lieutenant come almost invariably to mind. And also, since these
things could hardly be said better, his words:

> I was always embarrassed by the words sacred, glorious, and sacrifice and
> the expression in vain. We had heard them, sometimes standing in the
> rain almost out of earshot, so that only the shouted words came through
> . . . now for a long time, and I had seen nothing sacred, and the things
> that were glorious had no glory and the sacrifices were like the stockyards
> at Chicago if nothing was done with the meat except to bury it. . . .
> Abstract words such as glory, honor, courage, or hallow were obscene. . . .

It is on the implications of these sentiments, and in order to escape
a certain death which he has not deserved, that Henry finally acts.
He jumps in a river and deserts: the hell with it. It was an unforget-
table plunge.

Memorable too, in her devotion and her ordeal—though much less
memorable, and much less real—is Henry's English mistress. Idealized
past the fondest belief of most people, and even the more realistic
wishes of some, compliant, and bearing unmistakable indications of
the troubles to come when she will appear as mistress of heroes to

come, Catherine Barkley has at least some character in her own right, and is both the first true "Hemingway heroine," and the most convincing one. Completely real, once again and at once, are the minor characters—especially Rinaldi, the ebullient Italian doctor, and the priest, and Count Greffi, the ancient billiard player, and the enlisted ambulance drivers.

Chiefly, again, it is their speech which brings these people to life and keeps them living. The rest of the book, however, is less conversational in tone than before, and in other ways the writing is changed a little. The sentences are now longer, even lyrical, on occasion, and, once in a while, experimental, as Hemingway, not content to rest in the style that had made him already famous, tries for new effects, and does not always succeed. Taken as a whole, however, his prose has never been finer or more finished than in this novel. Never have those awesome, noncommittal understatements, which say more than could ever be written out, been more impressive. The book has passages which rate with the hardest, cleanest and most moving in contemporary literature.

The novel has one stylistic innovation that is important to it. This is the use of an object, rain, in a way that cannot be called symbolic so much as portentous. Hemingway had used water as a metaphoric purge of past experience before, and so Henry's emergence from the river into a new life, as from a total immersion, was not new. What is new in *A Farewell to Arms* is the consistent use of rain as a signal of disaster. Henry, in his practical realism, professes a disbelief in signs, and tells himself that Catherine's vision of herself dead in the rain is meaningless. But she dies in it and actually, glancing back at the end, one sees that a short, introductory scene at the very start of the book had presented an ominous conjunction of images—rain, pregnancy and death—which set the mood for all that was to follow, prefigured it and bound all the ends of the novel into a perfect and permanent knot.

This is really the old "pathetic fallacy" put to new use, and— since there is no need to take it scientifically or philosophically, but simply as a subtle and unobtrusive device for unity—quite an acceptable one, too. Good and bad weather go along with good and bad moods and events. It is not just that, like everyone, the characters respond emotionally to conditions of atmosphere, light and so on, but that there is a correspondence between these things and their fate. They win when it's sunny, and lose in the rain.

Thus, then, the weather, which as both omen and descriptive background (made once again to count for something) is a matter of style, cannot be extricated from the book's plot, or structure. This is of course built on the two themes involved in the ambiguity of "arms," which are developed and intensified together, with alternating emphasis, until at the extremity of one the hero escapes society, and the heroine everything. Despite the frequency with which they appear in the same books, the themes of love and war are really an unlikely pair, if not indeed—to judge from the frequency with which writers fail to wed them—quite incompatible. But in Hemingway's novel their courses run straight and exactly, though subtly, parallel, and he has managed to fuse them. In his affair with the war Henry goes from desultory participation to serious action and a wound, and then through his recuperation in Milan to a retreat which leads to his desertion. His relationship with Catherine Barkley undergoes six precisely corresponding stages—from a trifling sexual affair to actual love and her conception, and then through her confinement in the Alps to a trip to the hospital which leads to her death. By the end of Hemingway's novel, when the last farewell is taken, the two stories are as one, in the point that is made very clear, lest there be any sentimental doubt about it, that life, both social and personal, is a struggle in which the Loser Takes Nothing, either.

This ideology, which is the novel's, has two related aspects which are implicit in the united elements of the plot. In the end, a man is trapped. He is trapped biologically—in this case by the "natural" process that costs him his future wife in the harrowing scenes at the hospital, and is trapped by society—at the end of a retreat, where you take off or get shot. Either way it can only end badly, and there are no other ways. How you will get it, though, depends on the kind of person you are:

> If people bring so much courage to this world the world has to kill them to break them, so of course it kills them. The world breaks everyone and afterward many are strong at the broken places. But those that will not break it kills. It kills the very good and the very gentle and the very brave impartially. If you are none of these you can be sure that it will kill you too but there will be no special hurry.

It does not really matter very much that there is something a little romantic about this passage, perhaps the finest in all of Hemingway, or that the novel is a romantic one as a whole. It must be just about the most romantic piece of realistic fiction, or the most realistic romance, in our literature. Henry's love affair, which blossoms glamorously from the mud of the war, is but the most striking of several factors which go together to make his war a remarkably pleasant one, as wars go, and much more attractive than wars actually are. The lieutenant has a somewhat special time of it, with orderlies and porters and little or no trouble with superiors, and good wine and good food and a lot of free time in which to enjoy them. But it is not important that these aspects of his army experience are highly untypical. Nor does it matter on the other hand that women usually survive childbirth, and many men are discharged from armies in good shape, and then life goes on much as before. What matters instead is that this time Hemingway has made his story, and the attitudes it enacts, persuasive and compelling within the covers of his book. And after we have closed the covers there is no inclination to complain that this was, after all, no literal transcription of reality which exaggerated neither the bitter nor the sweet. It was rather an intensification of life. Willingly or not, disbelief is suspended before a vision that overrides objections, withers preconceptions and even memory and imposes itself in their place.

This novel has the last word, always. Catherine Barkley, as it happened, was very good, very gentle, very brave. Unlike the hero, who broke and survived to become eventually quite strong, she would not break and so she was killed. It was very likely in rebuttal to the people who rejected the pessimism of this denouement that Hemingway pointed out three years later, in *Death in the Afternoon,* that love stories do not end happily in life, either:

> There is no lonelier man in death, except the suicide, than that man who has lived many years with a good wife and then outlived her. If two people love each other there can be no happy end to it.

Learning to Care

by Earl Rovit

A Farewell to Arms is not generally regarded as an "epistemological story." It has been called among other things a "tragedy," an unconvincing romance, a masterful depiction of the impersonal cruelty of war. It may be some of these other things as well (although not, I think, a tragedy); but the key to its structure must lie in the lesson that the total experience has taught to Frederick Henry. It is his story which he tells in his own voice; the meanings which are sunk in the texture of the story can only be the meanings which he has recognized as salient in his experience because they offer him pragmatic hypotheses on what life *is* and, more important, who he *is*. The total effect of the story depends on the degree of Frederick's self-realization or acceptance of the implicit meanings in his experience; for, as we have seen with Hemingway, the identity of a man is measured by the processive recognitions of his meaningful experience. *A Farewell to Arms* departs slightly from the rigid format of the tutor–type structure in that there is no single tutor whom the tyro, Henry, will accept. There are, however, several tutors; and, in a sense, his entire series of episodic adventures is a composite tutorial stimulation.

The key to the motif of self-discovery occurs early in the novel when Frederick Henry attempts to explain to the priest and to himself why he had spent his furlough in the opiate-inducing carnival atmosphere of the cities rather than in the priest's home area, the Abruzzi:

> I myself felt as badly as he did and could not understand why I had not gone. It was what I had wanted to do and I tried to explain . . . winefully, how we did not do the things we wanted to do; we never did such things. . . . I had wanted to go to Abruzzi. I had gone to no place where the roads were frozen and hard as iron, where it was clear cold and dry and the snow was dry and powdery and hare-tracks in the snow and the peasants took off their hats and called you Lord and there was good hunting. I had gone to no such place but to the smoke of cafés and nights when the room whirled . . . nights in bed, drunk, when you knew that

"Learning to Care" (Editor's title). From Ernest Hemingway *by Earl Rovit (New York: Twayne Publishers, Inc., 1963), pp. 98–106. Copyrigh © 1963 by Twayne Publishers, Inc. Reprinted by permission of the publisher.*

that was all there was, and the strange excitement of waking . . . and
the world all unreal in the dark and so exciting that you must resume
again unknowing and not caring in the night, sure that this was all and
all and all and not caring. Suddenly to care very much and to sleep.
to wake with it sometimes morning and all that had been there gone and
everything sharp and hard and clear. . . . I tried to tell about the night
and the difference between the night and the day and how the night
was better unless the day was very clean and cold and I could not tell
it; as I cannot tell it now. But if you have had it you know. He had not
had it but he understood that I had really wanted to go to the Abruzzi
but had not gone and we were still friends, with many tastes alike, but
with the difference between us. *He had always known what I did not
know and what, when I learned it, I was always able to forget. But I did
not know that then, although I learned it later.* (13–14, italics added)

This lengthy excerpt is crucial, I believe, in outlining the frame of reference in which Frederick's experiences coalesce into a significant
shape. We must first know, of course, what he is before his experiences
begin; for it is only through measuring the distance between what he
had been and what he becomes that we can know what he is at the end
of the novel after he has finally learned what the priest had always
known. We must also remember that the complete novel is told in one
long memory-flashback; that there is a qualitative difference between
Henry the narrator–protagonist and Henry the actor–protagonist in
the novel. And that this difference—one in both time and knowledge
will necessarily impact a dynamic irony to the narrative perspective.

Frederick Henry's character at the beginning of the novel can be
readily summarized. He is rootless; he has a stepfather somewhere in
America, but he has quarrelled so much with his family that the only
communication between them is in their honoring of his sight drafts.
His general attitude toward life can be almost entirely abstracted from
the previously quoted excerpt. Most of the time he does not care about
anything at all: ". . . the world all unreal in the dark . . . and not
caring in the night, sure that this was all and all and all and not caring." He has been a student of architecture, but there is no indication
that this represents anything more than a casual easily dissolvable interest. He has volunteered to serve in the Italian Ambulance Corps for
reasons which are never made clear. He has neither patriotism nor
hatred of the Austrians. In fact, the war and his involvement in it are
as unreal experiences to him as anything else in his thoroughly meaningless and unconnected life. "Well, I knew I would not be killed. Not
in this war. It did not have anything to do with me. It seemed no more
dangerous to me myself than war in the movies" (39). Although he has
had sexual experiences with many women, none of them has lodged in
any meaningful way in the designing of his person. Or, to put it in
other terms, the character or *self–ness* of Frederick Henry which we

meet at the beginning of the novel is practically nonexistent. He *is* his
manners and his intermittent drive to satisfy his creature-instincts in
drinking, sex, and the sporadic excitement of the sensations which the
violence of war provides. And this central emptiness is brilliantly sym-
bolized in the persistent image of the masquerade; he is an unrooted
American disguised in an Italian uniform. Or, as Ferguson expertly
perceives when she calls him a "dirty sneaking American Italian," he is
"a snake with an Italian uniform: with a cape around [his] neck."

However, there is another aspect to his character to which the priest
responds. Although Henry represses and ignores it for the most part,
he does possess a strong potential "caringness." There are times, as we
see in the excerpt, when he cares a good deal; and everything becomes
"sharp and hard and clear." It is this aspect of his character which
grows during the novel and which serves as a force field for the development of his personality. However, in the beginning of the novel, and
up to the time of the wound, this aspect is consistently and consciously
smothered. "It was what I had wanted to do and I tried to explain . . .
winefully, how we did not do the things we wanted to do; we never
did such things. . . ." The careful adverb, "winefully," is the exposing
clue to the masquerade lie of Henry's protestations. It was *not* what he
had wanted to do at all. He *wanted* to go to the cities where he could
merge his excited emptiness into the empty carousings of a soldier's
leave in wartime. For one of the lessons that Henry learns in the course
of the novel is that people always do the things they want to do; and,
when their capacity for "caring" is limited or negligible, their wants
are most easily assuaged by passive activities of an instinctual nature.
Somewhat later in the novel when the characterization is no longer
completely true, Rinaldi acutely describes the Henry of emptiness:
"You are really an Italian," he says. "All fire and smoke and nothing
inside. You only pretend to be an American" (71).

Thus Henry is, in a sense, playing a double masquerade. He is to
Ferguson a sneaking American hiding in an Italian uniform; to
Rinaldi he is an Italian pretending to be an American. The ironies of
ambiguous identity will multiply at the bridge over the Tagliamento
when Henry will realize that to the battle police he will be "obviously
a German in Italian uniform." But at his second meeting with Catherine Barkley he is merely "not-caringness" willing to play the game
of caring if there is any prospect of an exciting reward; in other words,
his attitude toward her is precisely similar to his attitude toward the
war in general. We see this fact when she slaps him at the beginning
of their courtship: "I was angry and yet certain, seeing it all ahead like
the moves in a chess game." And then later he extends the game–playing metaphor, adding the disguise-motif: "I knew I did not love
Catherine Barkley nor had any idea of loving her. This was a game,

like bridge, in which you said things instead of playing cards. Like bridge you had to pretend you were playing for money or playing for some stakes. Nobody had mentioned what the stakes were. It was all right with me" (32).

In his incapacity to care he can, of course, play for any amount of stakes because he has nothing to lose. The wound is the first lesson to him of what he stands to lose. He realizes in the explosion of the trench-mortar shell that he does have a *me* that the war has something to do with: "I tried to breathe but my breath would not come and I felt myself rush bodily out of myself and out and out and out and all the time bodily in the wind. I went out swiftly, all of myself, *and I knew I was dead and it had all been a mistake to think you just died.* Then I floated, and instead of going on I felt myself slide back. I breathed and I was back" (58, italics added). The italicized segment is very curious; it seems to say that, in this moment of extreme shock, Henry realizes that he is dead and has been dead for a long time; and that the mistake is in thinking that he has just died. Such a reading would substantiate the thesis that Henry has lacked a *self* up to the time of the wound, because, in these terms, "not-caringness" is equivalent to death. But even if the italicized section is an awkwardness of construction, the effect of the nearness of death and the horror of the wound (the pain and the drip of the hemorrhaging corpse above him in the ambulance) is enough to indoctrinate that value of life which the fear of death must inevitably cause.

In the field hospital the issue is dramatically externalized in the successive visits of Rinaldi and the priest. Rinaldi, as he later describes himself, is "the snake of reason," or the rationalization of not-caringness; the priest is his opposite number, the dove of faith, the consecration of *caritas*. Rinaldi warns Frederick that love is an illusion when he perceives his friend's encroaching involvement with Catherine. He insists that he and Henry are similar inside; that neither of them entertains illusions (or "care"); hence, both are invulnerable. "I just tell you, baby, for your own good. To save you trouble." Henry does not accept the advice of his reason, but he does not reject it either.

With the arrival of the priest, the counter argument is delivered. The priest, filled with shame and disgust at the war, observes correctly that Frederick really doesn't mind the war. "You do not see it . . . even wounded you do not see it. I can tell." In the ensuing conversation the priest diagnoses Henry's deficiency and gives the definition of care which Henry will later come to embrace with qualifications:

He looked at me and smiled.
"You understand but you do not love God."
"No."

"You do not love Him at all?" he asked.
"I am afraid of him in the night sometimes."
"You should love Him."
"I don't love much."
"Yes," he said. "You do. What you tell me about in the nights. That is not love. That is only passion and lust. When you love you wish to do things for. You wish to sacrifice for. You wish to serve."
"I don't love" (76–77).

The issue has been drawn; and, although Frederick will come to a balance somewhere between Rinaldi and the priest, the rest of the novel will be an uninterrupted progress away from Rinaldi.

Book Two records the consummation of the affair with Catherine and the idyllic union they share in the four or so months of Henry's convalescence. According to the priest's definition of love, there is little doubt that Catherine achieves it: "I want just what you want. There isn't any me any more. Just what you want." But Henry's position is more difficult to determine. He "loves" Catherine, worries about not having married her when he learns that she is pregnant, and certainly enjoys her serviceable company. During his stay in the hospital, he centers on the island of pleasure and fulfillment which she fashions for him in the midst of the war. But his role is consistently that of the accepter of services; nowhere is there any indication that he is moved to become servitor as well as master. She creates the various "homes" they occupy, and at the termination of his treatment she remains outside the railway station, while he entrains to return to the front.

Book Three returns Frederick to the front and to the persuasive ministrations of his two friends, both of whom have fared badly under the strain of the summer offensives. Rinaldi fears that he has contracted syphilis (a traditional disease of lust); and, incapable of believing in anything not measurable by the empirical reason, he has buried himself in his work to avoid seeing the carnage and degradation that he works within. Henry is offered an insight into the inner life of his friend without illusions when Rinaldi, drunk, bitter, and a little hysterical tries to goad the priest into an argument: " 'No, no,' said Rinaldi. 'You can't do it. You can't do it. I say you can't do it. You're dry and you're empty and there's nothing else. There's nothing else I tell you. Not a damned thing. I know, when I stop working' " (185).

The priest, on the other hand, has also become depressed in his faith by the action of the war. He had believed in some kind of miracle which would intercede and cause men to lay down their arms, but now he has begun to doubt his belief. When he asks Frederick what he believes in, Frederick tells him, "In sleep." The answer receives an ironic doubling when Frederick apologizes: "I said that about sleeping, meaning nothing." The ironic slip may have been unconscious on Frederick's part, but it suggests that his capacity to care has not yet moved into the domain of the priest's definition.

The rest of Book Three takes Frederick into the Caporetto retreat, his vain attempt to save his ambulance crew and follow out his orders, and his climactic jump from the bridge into the Tagliamento. Yet his actions throughout this book still maintain the *passive*, moved–about quality that we observed in his character before his meeting with Catherine. He deserts at last, but only because he has been pushed to the wall. And, as he rides the flatcar to Mestre, he reflects: "I was not made to think. I was made to eat. My God, yes. Eat and drink and sleep with Catherine . . . and never going away again except together. Probably have to go damned quickly. She would go." There is probably a fractional move closer to a commitment to a *mutual* love relationship indicated here, but it should be noted that "the separate peace" is filed by Henry neither as an action through which he can rejoin his beloved, nor as an act of disillusionment with the ideals of war. As we saw earlier, he never had any of these ideals to start with; and we can suppose that, had there been no battle police on the bridge, he would not have left his unit at this time.

In Book Four, Frederick's course is confirmed. Moved by circumstances beyond his control, he accepts the consequences of his forced actions, among them the obligations of *caring* for Catherine in the priest's sense. On the train for Stresa, he feels like a "masquerader" in his civilian clothes, which is an ironic turnabout, because he is now going to Catherine as *himself* wholly for the first time. The extent to which he has allowed himself to be penetrated by his openness for her can be seen in the following reflection:

> Often a man wishes to be alone and a girl wishes to be alone too and if they love each other they are jealous of that in each other, but I can truly say we never felt that. We could feel alone when we were together, against the others. It has only happened to me like that once. I have been alone while I was with many girls and that is the way that you can be most lonely. But we were never lonely and never afraid when we were together. I know that the night is not the same as the day: that all things are different, that the things of the night cannot be explained in the day, because they do not then exist, and the night can be a dreadful time for lonely people once their loneliness has started. But with Catherine there was almost no difference in the night except that it was even better time (266–67).

In terms of the earlier discussion, the Frederick who meets Catherine at Stresa has gone to Abruzzi; and, in his caring, things have become "sharp and hard and clear" to him. Later in his conversation with the aged Count Greffi, he answers the latter's question as to what he values most by saying "Some one I love." And the Count, who is worried because he has not become devout in his old age, brings the priest's definition to bear on Frederick's new feeling when he tells him that his being in love is "a religious feeling." The game that Frederick had entered so blithely some six months before has become a game which he cannot back out of, and the stakes are very high. In the escape across the lake to Switzerland, the "separate peace" has become a separate "union," and the way is prepared for the fulfillment of Rinaldi's earlier prophecy that the "caring"–Henry would have a better time than he, but he would also suffer more remorse (181).

Book Five moves swiftly to its inevitable catastrophe. The interlude of waiting outside Montreux brings the separate "union" to its apotheosis; the move to Lausanne and the brilliantly handled hospital scenes leave Frederick Henry "saying good–by to a statue," which is all he has left of his gamble with love. In the rain, the persistent symbol of foreboding in the novel, he returns alone to his hotel, a winner who is taking nothing away from the gaming table but a "self" vulnerable to the hurts of the world. For we must realize that there are two opposite movements in the novel, and to neglect one of them is to throw the delicate ambiguity of the novel's balance awry. On the one hand, there is the current of doom—the inexorable march of tragic warning which is echoed in the imagery, the rain, and the narrator's prescient comments. It is this movement, presumably, which Hemingway must have been referring to when he termed *A Farewell to Arms* his *Romeo and Juliet*. And I suppose it is his *Romeo and Juliet,* although it bears very little resemblance to Shakespeare's. Frederick and Catherine do not fall in love at first sight; it is only very gradually that Frederick allows himself to be exposed to a real love; Catherine's death may be "a dirty trick," but it is not accidental; it is eminently natural. To compare Hemingway's lovers to those other "star–crossed" ones tells us little about Shakespeare and forces an unjust criticism of Hemingway's more limited success.

For the other movement in the novel is one in which there is no precedent in Shakespeare's tragedy. Frederick Henry establishes a connection with the world in his love affair with Catherine and, in so doing, becomes humanly alive. That she dies does not negate his experience; it pushes him into the position of the Major who also had trouble in resigning himself. Frederick moves from the safety of the half–man who has found things that he cannot lose, to the precarious and highly vulnerable position of the man who has made an investment in life and must learn to back his play. And that he does learn to resign himself is obvious in the fact that it is he, not an impersonal narrator, who tells the story. As is the case with "In Another Country," Hemingway does not spell out the process of adjustment that Frederick goes through in order to learn to endure his loss. He leaves the significant facts in the narrative structure; they are there because the narrator Frederick has abstacted them from the actor Frederick's experience. And these tell us that Frederick does not return to the Rinaldi position where there is nothing but emptiness and dryness underneath; nor does he embrace the faith of the priest. He accepts the reality of the naturalistic world in which death is a fact every bit as real as sex; but he also accepts the reality of a love which he helped to create, and this fact is also as real as death. And, as a final gloss on the novel, we may find a small substantiation in the title. *A Farewell to Arms* is beautifully ambiguous in two obvious realms: the farewell to war in the separate peace, the farewell to the beloved in death. But it also may suggest a farewell to those arms which the early Frederick Henry had opposed to the world: a farewell to "not–caringness" which gives a death–in–life to which no one can resign himself.

The Tough Romance

by Robert W. Lewis, Jr.

In the first chapter, Hemingway's early period was divided from his middle and transitional period at the point of Catherine Barkley's death, the event that concludes *A Farewell to Arms*. A common technique of fiction complicates the discussion of this novel in relation to Hemingway's ideas about and dramatization of love, and that technique is the use of Frederic Henry as the first-person narrator.[1] If one reads his story without understanding the direction that the first–person narration gives it, one may very well come to a far different conclusion from the point that Hemingway is making.

While it is true that Catherine's death concludes the novel, her death is really only the end of a beginning as far as Frederic Henry is concerned; he is now ready to reflect on his recent experiences and to present them to the reader, and he is a very sophisticated narrator. He is not merely recounting events in an objective way. (If he were, the advantage of the first-person over a third-person point of view would be questionable.) Like many of the protagonists of the short stories and like Jake Barnes, another first-person narrator, Henry has undergone an initiatory and learning experience that he is now ready to interpret. The wonderful sense of immediacy that Henry can convey in this most brilliantly written of Hemingway's novels should not mislead the reader into thinking that the events transpire and are immediately recorded in a diary or epistolary form.

Nor is Henry a naive innocent like a Huckleberry Finn; he looks back on his adventures but without conveying the degree of understanding that Twain, through brilliant use of an ironic "unreliable" narrator, enabled the reader to experience. The vividness of scene and dialogue in *A Farewell to Arms* is countered by the heavy and carefully prepared feeling of doom that makes us see Henry the narrator

---

"The Tough Romance." From Hemingway on Love by Robert W. Lewis, Jr. (Austin: University of Texas Press, 1965), pp. 39–54. Copyright © 1965 by Robert W. Lewis, Jr. Reprinted by permission of the publisher.

[1] Earl Rovit, *Ernest Hemingway* (pp. 98–106), has come to similar conclusions about the meaning of the novel as determined by the point of view. [See this volume, pp. 33–40.]

as strangely detached from and lifeless in the vivid world that he can nonetheless evoke around his immediate past, the subject of his story. His past catatonic state is a brilliant anachronism: all the events that have created his sense of loss and isolation have already occurred when he begins the presentation of his story, and each scene that he re-creates for us is distorted by the climactic event of Catherine's death at the end of the novel.

For example, in the mess-hall scenes of Chapters 2 and 3, Henry is set apart from his messmates superficially by his nationality but profoundly by his "tragic" experience, but it is an experience that has not yet happened. His isolation is anachronistic in that he creates the feeling of it by his hindsight into the scenes, just as he "remembers" in Chapter 1 that the soldiers marching to their deaths looked as though they were pregnant (an image that foreshadows, of course, Catherine's death in childbirth). Throughout the novel, Henry uses rain and Catherine's feelings about the rain in the same portentous way. (She sees herself dead in it, and sure enough—) Unlike Huck Finn, Frederic Henry is thus demonstrated to be terribly literary. The clinching passage comes early in the novel and justifiably should arouse the reader's curiosity, as it indirectly informs him that Henry has undergone a learning experience that he is now reflecting on and writing about. In an initially cryptic comment Henry says that the priest in his outfit

> had always known what I did not know and what, when I learned it, I was always able to forget. But I did not know that then, although I learned it later.[2]

What is the "it" he learned but the entire initiatory experience with war and death, Catherine and love that the novel is about? The pattern of the novel, like that of *Adventures of Huckleberry Finn,* is of the narrator's sequential exposure to evil, but unlike Huck Finn (whose "reversion" to adolescence in the last third of the novel many critics do not like), Frederic Henry becomes aware of the nature of the evil that exists around and within him.[3] Henry *thinks* more and more as the novel progresses, though sometimes he thinks against his will because some things, as Joseph Conrad's Winnie Verloc put it, do not bear much looking into. The meaning of the novel must be inherent in the pattern and, again like *Huckleberry Finn,* it involves many disguises and frequent reversals of the expected.[4] In Chapter 1 the disguise motif is set most importantly in the figure of the soldiers

[2] Ernest Hemingway, *A Farewell to Arms*, p. 14. Subsequent references to this novel in this chapter will be in the text itself.

[3] Cf. Philip Young, *Ernest Hemingway*, Ch. 6, for an extension of the relation of Huckleberry Finn to the Hemingway hero.

[4] Rovit (*Ernest Hemingway*, pp. 100–101) also cites the disguise motif.

who look as if they were pregnant, but it is also present in the literal camouflaging of the mechanized instruments of doom, the big tractor–drawn guns that are disguised by the growth of life, "green leafy branches and vines" (3). This irony is implicit in Henry's view of the war: when seven thousand soldiers die of cholera, he says that "only" seven thousand died (4), and towns are captured "handsomely," and the destructive war is "going well" (5–6).

Images of camouflage enlarge to reinforce a number of ironies central to the theme. Identities are confused, roles are exchanged, motives are misunderstood, and deceit, hypocrisy, and phoniness are rife in a succession of dramatic ironies: Henry is an American in Italian uniform; he pretends to love Catherine, who substitutes him for her dead fiancé; the whole war is theatrical and ridiculous (Chapter 6); Henry learns that some patriots, some singers, and some doctors are phonies (Chapters 15 and 19); he and Catherine conceal their lovemaking in the hospital as he conceals the empty wine and liquor bottles that he accumulates (Chapters 16 and 22); they go to a "fixed" horse race, which has symbolic overtones of a fixed love, especially in view of Hemingway's frequent use of the horse as an erotically symbolic beast (Chapter 20); the two virgin sisters misunderstood Aymo's Italian and his gestures (Chapter 28); in the disaster at Caporetto the Italians greatly fear Germans who have been rumored to be dressed in Italian uniforms, and the battle police are summarily trying and executing their own officers (as Henry had himself shot an Italian sergeant) while the Germans—the enemy—are attacking without any resistance (Chapters 27–30); after his escape from the battle police, Henry disguises himself first as an enlisted man, then as a civilian (Chapters 32–33), and as a civilian he "felt [like] a masquerader" (260); after his reunion with Catherine, they use deceit to escape to Switzerland and there pass themselves off first as cousins and then as a married couple (Chapters 36–37); masked like a doctor, Henry watches helplessly as in the final reversal, the act of birth ends in death (Chapter 41).

All these ironies, reversals, and disguises are metaphors and preparation for Henry's disillusionment—first with the war which he had presumably volunteered to be in, and second with his romance with Catherine, which, to give him credit, he had not initially volunteered for. An intrinsic though literary precedent within the details of the narrative has thus been set for the reader to perceive the tendency and effect of Henry as an extraordinary kind of narrator.

Though it is perhaps easy to accept the idea of an ironic or unreliable narrator or a narrator who tells about a radical change in his own character, in practice the convention is sometimes deceptive, and Hemingway's use of it here has probably caused many misreadings of the love theme in the novel. One such misunderstanding is reflected in

Edmund Wilson's passing comments on the novel.[5] He calls it a tragedy in which the lovers are innocent victims, and this view he supports through reference to Hemingway's own comment that *A Farewell to Arms* was a *Romeo and Juliet.* Perhaps having read *A Farewell to Arms* not too sympathetically, Wilson gives evidence of never having read *Romeo and Juliet,* or at least of subscribing rather carelessly to the popular notions of what that play is about. In light of Hemingway's remark, a cursory examination of some parallelisms in the works may be instructive. As Wilson says, both pairs of lovers are star–crossed, but are they tragic? Without further worrying that problem of whether tragedy is possible today or is ever possible in the genre of the novel, one can certainly see the qualitative difference between *Romeo and Juliet* and Shakespeare's great tragedies. Further, Romeo lacks tragic self-awareness; Mercutio with his antiromantic wit keeps the play from slopping over; and even Juliet hints at Shakespeare's realization of the foolishness of the conventions of romantic love. And yet the play can quite rightly be considered as the first great expression of romantic love in English literature. Likewise *A Farewell to Arms* can be wept over —it is truly moving, but largely, I suspect, because most of us have had our sensibilities trained to be moved almost automatically by such stuff. But we also see with Mercutio's eyes (or Rinaldi's and the priest's in the novel) while we *feel* with Romeo's whole being.

Wilson's view is very well, as far as it goes, but Wilson thinks of *A Farewell to Arms* as a limited success because of the flatness or conventionality of the characterizations, a view that indicates that he regards the Frederic Henry of the action of the novel as the same Frederic Henry who is the later narrator. The distinction is crucial for a fair view of Hemingway's skill. Appreciation of this manipulation of point of view doesn't mean that Hemingway has here discovered his love ethic, because the novel is like *The Sun Also Rises* in being negative, a novel of disillusionment that holds only slight hope for the future of a character like Frederic Henry. Thus these two readings of *A Farewell to Arms* are possible, but neither is wholly right by itself. My comments here assume Henry's growing awareness of the emptiness of romance, but the moralist in me despises the earlier, ignorant protagonist; and even at the end of the novel his knowledge is felt rather than intellectualized. Always, however, the important distinction must be remembered that Hemingway is not Henry. While one may deliberately criticize the "ethic" of Frederic Henry, the more impassioned the abuse, the greater the implication of the success, in a technical sense, of Hemingway's novel. The reader becomes completely absorbed and perhaps

[5] Edmund Wilson, "Hemingway: Gauge of Morale," *The Wound and the Bow.* Leslie A. Fiedler, *Love and Death in the American Novel,* gives another brilliant misreading (p. 306) because he assumes the complete Ernestness of Frederic Henry.

partisan, either for romance or against it. (And I strongly suspect the judgment of those readers who admire the "emotional impact" of the "love" story. It is a very good novel, but for reasons other than those that Hollywood periodically capitalizes on by producing screen versions of it.)

Chronologically the novel is a flashback in the life history of the Hemingway hero. Frederic Henry is not, of course, Jake Barnes, but he bears many similarities to him, as Philip Young has pointed out. Assuming some continuity between the Hemingway heroes, can one also assume that the protagonist of *A Farewell to Arms* is not only younger but also less mature in his "love ethic," or does the younger hero represent an advancing stage in the development of Hemingway's changing views of love? Perhaps it is best to read *A Farewell to Arms* simply as a complementary, little-changed view of love. The second novel does not repeat the views of the first novel but fills in with different emphases Hemingway's earlier statement. Both *The Sun Also Rises* and this second novel closely parallel T. S. Eliot's *The Waste Land*. There is the emphasis on the seasons and the contrast between natural cycles and symbols and the human cycle of disjointed activities. And just as we can imagine Jake as an older Lieutenant Henry, so do we note that Brett Ashley shares with Catherine her Circe-like powers to ruin her lover. One general difference even strengthens the connection and may be thought of as the difference between Hemingway's epic knight (Jake) and his chivalric knight (Henry). The former held the manly virtues of courage, strength, and loyalty in highest esteem; the latter admired love and gentleness. *The Sun Also Rises* is Hemingway's *chanson de geste,* in which the the action and love are violent and the "women are often inclined to evil and always burning with desire while the men are by nature temperate and businesslike." [6]

In general outline, *A Farewell to Arms* is chivalric in its emphasis on the love story, though war provides the background and Hemingway moves back and forth between those strange but time-honored bedcompanions, love and war. Against his will, a young officer falls deeply in love with a beautiful nurse—the scenario goes. The horrors of war are contrasted with the wonders of love, but in the end Death the master reaches the hero, who thought he had escaped death by escaping the war. Ironically, it is through love that he is hurt. Still, love is better than war.

But this slightly absurd summary is by no means a complete statement of the essence of the novel that is, rather, about another confusion and distortion of values and love—as in *The Sun Also Rises,* in which the reader does not have to condone the hero and heroine's ac-

[6] Maurice Valency, *In Praise of Love,* p. 54.

tions though he must become emotionally involved in their human condition. Also like *The Sun Also Rises, A Farewell to Arms* is one of the best written of Hemingway's books. It is in an examination of the attitudes of the chief characters—but not perhaps of Hemingway's attitudes—that the reader is frustrated and annoyed. *A Farewell to Arms* hints at the understanding of the values of agape that are to emerge gradually, but its hero and heroine are still mired in the follies and contradictions of "true love." The follies are not as apparent as in *The Sun Also Rises.* The toughness is so deluding that Hemingway seems already to have begun to move from romanticism to agape. But as Joseph Warren Beach has seen: "Hemingway, in his severely 'modern' and unromantic idiom, has given us a view of love as essentially romantic as any of his predecessors in the long line of English novelists." [7]

Beach, however, is generally pleased with the view, "romance" carrying no onus for him. He describes the story as an embodiment of the transcendental values of courage and love, a love neither irresponsible nor one that ends sentimentally or melodramatically. Beach's reasoning is that Catherine Barkley and Lieutenant Henry do plan to marry after the child is born, and their love is sealed by death and suffering if not by marriage vows. Further, if there is any bad love in the story, it is the "whorehouse love" which symbolizes the evil of war. Humane love is impossible under the conditions of war, Beach says, ignoring the wartime love of Robert Jordan and Maria in *For Whom the Bell Tolls.*[8]

In the light of subtle but undeniable evidence in the novel itself, one cannot hold with these views, even though they are tempting to espouse, largely because they coincide with congenital clichés and flatter hard-to-shake ideas about the nobility of romantic love. As Maurice Valency describes it, romantic love is an amatory fixation on a single ideal, and it centers on the courtship stage of a relationship.[9] On the surface of this love, the romantic appears to be concerned only with pleasing his love object.

Within a tough context of modern war not fought according to chivalric rules, the love affair in *A Farewell to Arms* is wildly romantic. An improbable hero and heroine live an adolescent dreamlife full of adventure and sex. When the courtship is over (when Catherine is pregnant), she conveniently dies, as does the baby who would have been so troublesome to the hero. Iseults never have babies. Lieutenant Frederic Henry falls into a love trap. Initially he says he wants only physical love, and Catherine is preferable to the whores in the army-sponsored bordello whom Henry visited regularly and who might give him another case of gonorrhea. Catherine is, after all, beautiful to him (18)

[7] Joseph Warren Beach, *American Fiction: 1920–1940,* p. 88.
[8] *Ibid.,* pp. 85–89.
[9] Valency, *In Praise of Love,* pp. 17–18.

and eminently available, working at the field hospital where he is attached and being "a little crazy" because of the death of her soldier fiancé.

But this knight who had never been in love and who knew he "did not love Catherine Barkley nor had any idea of loving her" (32) swiftly changes his mind. Suddenly the ribaldry of the officers' mess and the romanceless love of the whorehouse is distasteful to him, and he regrets having treated Catherine so lightly. Away from her he feels "lonely and empty," "lonely and hollow" (44). After his wounding—the beginning of the end of his romance with war—Catherine comes to his hospital bed, and "When I saw her I was in love with her" (98). Tristan and Iseult fell in love after drinking a magic love potion. For Henry the magic lay perhaps in Catherine's long blonde hair that he admires so much (19, 27, 276, 312–313, 320, 324).[10]

Henry falls in love hard, but it is interesting to note that he repeats the imagery of "lonely and empty," "lonely and hollow" in quite different contexts. In *To Have and Have Not* this image of emptiness or hollowness becomes a major sign of the lonely and loveless man. One would think that Henry lost his loneliness when he fell in love with Catherine, but subsequent uses of the imagery suggest that she does not quite satisfy his spiritual hunger. After a night of love with her he feels "hollow and hungry" (167) though admittedly the hunger is literally for food. After his escape from the battle police, he feels "hollow and sick," "lonesome inside and alone," seeing things "clearly and emptily" (243, 247–248); he has made his separate peace, and perhaps this hollowness and emptiness is a foretaste of his later not altogether happy isolation with Catherine. After his reunion with her, Henry says that they never wished to be separated from each other as ordinary mortal lovers sometimes wish privacy, but he adds that they were "alone against the others" (266), that their separate peace had left them (or at least Henry) with no defense except each other. Still later, Catherine apologizes to Henry because their "marriage" has limited his activities. He had tried to keep from thinking, and he answers:

"My life used to be *full* of everything. . . . Now if you aren't with me I haven't a thing in the world. . . ."

"*Don't think* about me when I'm not here."

"That's the way I worked it at the front. But there was something to do then."

"Othello with his occupation gone," she teased.

". . . I'm not jealous. I'm just so in love with you that there isn't anything else." (274; my emphasis)

[10] J. Huizinga, *The Warning of the Middle Ages,* p. 91. Huizinga refers to the magical power attributed to hair in the chivalric code.

We are moved by this loneliness to pity Henry rather than to envy him
for the realization of what he thought he longed for.

Other evidence in the novel indicates an understanding of the folly
of the romantic view of life. Initially it is not with Catherine that
Henry sees folly, but with the war, that other aspect of his current life.
In addition to the disguise and reversal motif, there is the well-known
passage in which Henry tells of his embarrassment "by the words
sacred, glorious, and sacrifice" (196); Hemingway indicates his disillusionment with war as a noble enterprise. Catherine, too, had had romantic notions about war which, like her fiancé, were all blown to bits
by reality (20). The "theatrical" war on the "picturesque" Italian front
with its noble leaders is a fraud. Toilet paper and a gas mask are more
useful than a sword and pistol (29–30, 38–9, 159).

It is one thing to see the mud, pain, sickness, and death of war, and
another thing to retreat from an illusion of it to an illusion of escape in
those other arms, the arms of a goddess, as Rinaldi the cynical surgeon
calls Catherine (71). Henry's escape involves more than a rejection of
war; it more seriously entails a loss of agape, both literally and symbolically. In Chapter 1, Henry writes in the first-person plural: he is
part of a group. But as the war goes badly and he grows increasingly
bitter and restless, his point of view becomes personal. Immediately
after first making love with Catherine, Henry is divorced from his role
as a participant in the war by his severe wounding. When Catherine is
transferred to Henry's rear-echelon hospital, he resumes the "we" point
of view once more, but he means in this later case just Catherine and
himself, no one else. He is isolated from mankind, and it is but a short
step further to the "separate peace" that he declares, knowing full well
that it will make him "damned lonely" until he can return to Catherine. Of course, the separate peace is well motivated: Henry will likely
be shot as a spy if he does not escape from the singleminded Italian
battle police. But after this immediate aversion of a foolish, undeserved
fate, Henry continues to run—from war and its commitment to others
and to vague, often hypocritical ideals, and its difficult decisions and
responsibilities (Henry had shot an Italian sergeant who had refused
to help get his ambulances out of the mud). He runs to the simplicity,
isolation, and irresponsibility of an idyllic life with his beloved.

And this beloved is a woman who has no self and very little depth
as a fictional character. Whether Hemingway could or could not create
a lifelike woman character (a question that is often argued) seems beside the point here and elsewhere in his fiction. He had no need for one
in a context that demanded a heroine who lacked a self (and lacking a
self does not at all mean being selfless). Selfhood or individuality is necessary for one to love and be loved or to be selfless, but Catherine is
afraid of herself in a manner that suggests Nick Adams' fear of falling

asleep after his traumatic wounding; the background of her fear was the violent death of her first fiancé and her subsequent "craziness." She wants to lose her identity in her lover. She doesn't care what they do or where they go; whatever Henry wants is fine with her; she will be what he wants, and they will never fight because if anything ever came between them they would "be gone"; she doesn't "live at all" when they are apart even briefly, and once after seeing a fox she imagines how lovely it would be for them to be in such a nonhuman condition where thought and individuality would be even more remote than in their Swiss hideout (146, 148–149, 320, 323).

It is to Henry's credit that his solution is felt to be suspect. The lovers have everything their own way up to the very end of the story, but their lives are marred, and not simply by the premonition and foreshadowing of death. They flee Italy and guarantee their safety in Switzerland by a rowboat escape that parallels Tristan and Iseult's honeymoon cruise, but the honeymoon is over for Henry whether he knows it or not. The barriers to their happiness have been met and overcome: Catherine's "craziness" about her dead fiancé, Miss Van Camp (the unsympathetic head nurse), the war itself, Henry's wound, finally even the soldiers of the country Henry served.

The love of Tristan and Iseult feeds on suffering and obstacles; without them, there is no love. And in spite of what Henry says, his solution to the war has been to reject love in the ordinary sense of friendship and kindness. From Tristan and Iseult to Antony and Cleopatra to Frederic and Catherine—living for romantic love is personal and a rejection of the larger, more magnanimous, more perilous agape. In such contexts, the two loves are antithetical. There is a pseudotragic ring to the ending, for in the depths of his mind Henry is really glad that Catherine dies, yet there is a metaphorical appropriateness to the ending, for as a story of self versus antiself, with a movement from commitment to desertion and death, the novel can be read as an exemplary one. Romantic love is not the solution to war or any other human dilemma.

As in *The Sun Also Rises*, the conclusion is negative, but in *A Farewell to Arms* there are more hints of a positive solution than there were in *The Sun Also Rises*. In Henry's friendship with Rinaldi and the priest attached to the army hospital, he finds human affections that are not unrealistic. The fact that he deserts these friends in making his separate peace is merely a sign of Henry's confusion, for he cannot satisfy his longings through them. Both Rinaldi and the priest are in some measure sick of the war too. Rinaldi finds his relief in whores and liquor; the priest clings to his faith and his love of his simple mountain homeland in Abruzzi. They take different medicines, but neither quits, neither reaches the turning point that Henry does, and each has a different view of the love between man and woman (Rinaldi's: 71–72, 179–186; the priest's: Chapter 11, 188–189).

The idea that Henry's decision has not been the best possible one is hinted at as early as Chapter 20, when he and Catherine are fully committed to each other and supposedly living in erotic bliss while he is recuperating from his wounds. At Catherine's suggestion, they leave their friends at a racetrack in order to be by themselves.

The ironic overtones of their conversation seem unmistakable. Just because they bet on an unknown and losing horse (when they could have had the name of the winner from the shady Mr. Meyers), Catherine illogically feels "cleaner." Henry's voice is quiet, and Catherine, who orders some drinks, has assumed the active, male role. He is reduced to banalities like "It's grand here" and "It's nice" as Catherine has him cornered and all to herself. But apparently she is sensitive to his controlled restiveness, for she soon says, " 'Don't let me spoil your fun, darling. I'll go back whenever you want.' " He indulges her, at least until they can finish their drinks, and she is grateful, but the last sentences of the episode are beautifully instructive of the inherent dullness of his life with her: "After we had been alone awhile we were glad to see the others again. We had a good time" (141). Such stylistic flatness belies Henry's statement and gives it an ironic twist. Of course he has had enough of a certain kind of excitement in the war to appreciate a near vacuum of intellectual stimulation, and the nocturnal crestings of his passion must alternate with such troughs of sensation. But there is the tonal hint that Henry has already seen what the realization of romance is like. And by its nature romance cannot be domesticated.

In Book V, after the last obstacle to their peace has been surmounted —they have perilously escaped to Switzerland just before Henry was to have been arrested for desertion—the lovers are so happy that they are bound to be bored, just as Henry had earlier been bored by the kind priest whom he had, nonetheless, liked (8–9, 145). The priest had urged Henry to go to his home in Abruzzi, where men still loved each other. The vision of goodness was attractive to Henry, but he had perversely refused to go there where the land was frozen, the air cold and dry, the peasants kind, and the hunting good. Instead of in this good place purified by the white snow, he had spent his leave in drunken whoring, which he had certainly enjoyed, but he had to face himself alone in the daytime, as he faces Catherine at the racetrack without the blinding stimulation of blind eros or the narcotic of drunkenness. His world was "all unreal in the dark and so exciting." The "night was better" than the day "unless the day was very clean and cold" like the days in Abruzzi. Henry tries to explain to his friend the priest why he had not visited the priest's homeland, but he cannot—for he himself does not quite know why.

He had always known what I did not know, and what, when I learned it, I was always able to forget. But I did not know that then, although I learned it later. (13–14)

The confusion of eros and the dissatisfaction with it are clear, but Henry never returns to this cryptic comment to say what it was he later learned. Yet if the central story is one of a farewell to arms that turns out badly, one can assume that that farewell was an unfortunate decision. Henry describes a number of little encounters with real people who are both good and bad and who intermittently establish him in a social milieu. There are a street artist (143–144), Meyers and his wife (Chapters 19–20), the hospital porter and his wife who cries when Henry leaves (156), a hotel manager (167), the captain of artillery to whom Henry gives his seat on the train (169–170), the two stray sergeants whom Henry at least has the social involvement to hate and even kill (217–218), his Italian ambulance crew and especially his driver Aymo whom he "had liked as well as anyone" he ever knew (229), the singer Simmons who gives him some clothes (257–259), and the barman in Stresa who is an old friend and helps him escape (Chapter 36). Along with Rinaldi and the priest, the doctors and nurses, and Count Greffi, these minor characters help describe the actual world of little victories and defeats that so sharply contrast with Henry and Catherine's Wagnerian world.

Mixed in with the quiet scenes of their mountain happiness, in Book V, are the undercurrents of the same malaise that touched Henry at the racetrack. He is distracted. Repeatedly he turns his mind back to the war that he had so conclusively left; time after time he picks up the newspapers to read about the war, even when Catherine is in the hospital having her difficult delivery (311, 312, 328, 330, 331, 341, 352). And he admits that sometimes he wonders about the front and people he knows there. He tells the curious Catherine at one moment that he is thinking about nothing, but on being pressed, he says he was thinking about Rinaldi and whether he had syphilis (319).

A curious contradiction of statements and actions develops that is almost painful to read if one senses the waning of the romance. Of course, the loss of idyllic love is no loss at all if it is exchanged for a realistic, conscious harmony of the lovers, but one wonders how deeply Henry understands his own honesty. And that is what is painful—the honesty that permits the hero to reveal the secret unrest that the Tristan feels when he no longer suffers for love. That there is a contradiction between the open expression and the secret expression of Henry's feelings is not hypocrisy; it is rather a dimension of characterization that is seldom realized, and whether or not Hemingway was conscious of what he was doing—as one may feel Henry is not fully conscious—the portrayal is a brilliant tour de force in manipulating point of view.

For example, the slow-moving Book V pictures Catherine and Henry as a happy couple enjoying a well appointed if not luxurious holiday in Switzerland. To Henry, Catherine is a "lovely wife" (314) to whom he says, "Oh, darling, I love you so" (313). Yet he senses trouble in paradise (314–316, 332), and Catherine (with the reader) senses restlessness in him (318–319). His premonitions might very well be instigated by boredom as much as by the desire for new barriers to their love. In any event, they have little to do but express love for one another and their mutual dependence. The canker is subtly depicted:

> "Let's go to sleep at exactly the same moment" [Catherine said].
> "All right."
> But we did not. I was awake for quite a long time thinking about things and watching Catherine sleeping, the moonlight on her face. Then I went to sleep, too. (321)

The "things" Henry thinks of are presumably the war and his friends who have not made their separate peace. Yet when Catherine asks him if he wants to see other people, he flatly answers "no"—the lovers are dependent on each other, but independent of the world; even their baby will not come between them (323).

Henry has attempted to reduce life to its lowest denominator, to make it simple, to make it thoughtless, to destroy consciousness and responsibility in a romantic, orgiastic dream. He does not even want to think of his family because it will make him worry about them (324). But now Iseult is pregnant and possessive. She wishes to consume Henry in destructive love; after the birth " 'You'll fall in love with me all over again,' " Catherine says.

> "Hell," I said, "I love you enough now. What do you want to do? Ruin me?"
> "Yes. I want to ruin you."
> "Good," I said, "that's what I want too." (325)

The dramatic situation does not support an image of happiness. The passage "We had a fine life. We lived through the months of January and February and the winter was very fine and we were very happy" (326) clearly seems ironical, though at that time Henry may have wanted to believe what he said.

During Catherine's difficult delivery Henry thinks of love as a biological trap. Nature is giving Catherine hell, not some deity who is punishing them for illicit love, he thinks. Yet he prays, and the idea of retribution is in his mind. Thinking of the child as a "by-product of good nights in Milan" seems a deliberately casual front for doubt and guilt (342). When he administers anesthetic gas to Catherine, he says of the gauge that he is "afraid of the numbers above two" (345). Literally, he does not want to give Catherine too much gas; metaphorically, he is afraid of the complications the baby will introduce to his simple life, just as he was afraid and yet drawn to the complications of the war—the multiplicity of responsibility, the lack of clear-cut issues, the meaning within meaninglessness, as with the taboo words *sacred* and *glorious*.

Catherine and the baby die. She is killed in the biological trap. As she is drained of her life's blood, Henry too feels an emptying inside of him, a feeling of the hollowness that Jake Barnes had felt and that will grow into a major image for loveliness and loneliness in the pivotal novel *To Have and Have Not*. One's sympathy for Henry is genuine, but it is tempered by the intellectual reservation that he was not, after all, prepared for growth beyond romantic love. He was not psychically ready to be a father and a husband. His last conversation with Catherine is sticky, bitter, and sad:

> "Do you want me to get a priest or any one to come and see you?"
> "Just you," she said. . . .
> "You won't do our things with another girl, or say the same things, will you?"
> "Never."
> "I want you to have girls, though."
> "I don't want them."
> "You are talking too much," the doctor said. "Mr. Henry must go out. He can come back again later. You are not going to die. You must not be silly."
> "All right," Catherine said. "I'll come and stay with you nights," she said. (354)

Their love is hermetic and ritualized, and eros is not central to it (conveniently, one suspects, for the hero's sake: he can enjoy his agony and also an occasional romp).

Catherine is a hard-to-believe dream girl who can be read on the realistic level only as a neurotic but who is better read as a deliberate stylization. Her death carries the hope with it of the destruction of her destructive love that excludes the world, that in its very denial of self possesses selfishly, that leads nowhere beyond the bed and the dream of a mystical transport of ordinary men and women to a divine state of love through foolish suffering. Indeed, the doctor and both of them say that it is foolish and silly to die. But die Catherine does, and the emptiness that Henry feels is the necessary state that must precede a refilling of his spirit with the more substantial stuff of agape. The old love dies with Catherine, and Henry's malaise even when living his idyll before her death is practically a guarantee that the Hemingway hero, having tried one love that has failed, will search for another. The promise of success had been hinted at in the first two novels. It was to be gradually evolved in Hemingway's middle period.

Symposium on Sensibility and/or Symbol in *A Farewell to Arms*

Malcolm Cowley: Rain as Disaster

. . . In *A Farewell to Arms,* the rain becomes a conscious symbol of disaster. "Things went very badly," the hero tells us in the first chapter. "At the start of the winter came the permanent rain and with the rain came the cholera." Catherine Barkley is afraid of the rain because, she says, "sometimes I see me dead in it." Rain falls all during the retreat from Caporetto; it falls while Catherine is trying to have her baby in a Swiss hospital; and it is still falling when she dies and when Frederic pushes the nurses out of the room to be alone with her. "It wasn't any good," he says. "It was like saying goodbye to a statue. After a while I went out and left the hospital and walked back to the hotel in the rain." On the other hand, it is snow that is used as a symbol of death in "The Snows of Kilimanjaro" (along with other death symbols, like vultures, hyenas, and soaring in an imaginary airplane). And possibly snow has the same value in *For Whom the Bell Tolls,* where a spring snowfall adds to the danger of Robert Jordan's mission and indirectly causes his death.

Even in these later novels and stories, Hemingway almost never makes the error that weakens the effect of most symbolic fiction. Ordinarily we think of it as a type of writing in which the events in the foreground tend to become misty because the author has his eyes fixed on something else. Hawthorne, in *The Marble Faun,* was so preoccupied with inner meanings that he seemed to lose his sense of the real world; but that is almost never the case with Hemingway. It is true that Maria, in *For Whom the Bell Tolls,* is almost more of a dream than she is a woman. When Frederic Henry dives into the flooded Tagliamento, in *A Farewell to Arms,* he is performing a rite of baptism that prepares us for the new life he is about to lead as a deserter from the Italian army; his act is emotionally significant, but it is a little unconvincing on the plane of action. These are perhaps the only two cases in which

"Rain as Disaster" (Editor's title). From "Introduction" to The Portable Hemingway, *ed. Malcolm Cowley (New York: The Viking Press, Inc., 1944), p. 16. Copyright 1944 by The Viking Press, Inc. Reprinted by permission of the publisher.*

Hemingway seems to loosen his grip on reality. Elsewhere his eyes are fixed on the foreground; but he gives us a sense of other shadowy meanings that contribute to the force and complexity of his writing.

Louis L. Martz: The Unreferable Rain

This sense of a double vision at work in tragedy is somewhat akin to I. A. Richards' famous variation on Aristotle, where Richards finds the essence of tragedy to reside in a "balanced poise." In the "full tragic experience," Richards declares, "there is no suppression. The mind does not shy away from anything." But Richards himself, like Hemingway's hero, then proceeds to shy away from transcendental matters, when he declares that the mind, in tragedy, "stands uncomforted, unintimidated, alone and self-reliant." This, it seems, will not quite square with Richards' ultimate account of tragedy as "perhaps the most general, all-accepting, all-ordering experience known."

A clearer account, at least a more dogmatic account, of this double vision of tragedy has been set forth by Joyce in his *Portrait of the Artist.* "Aristotle has not defined pity and terror," says Stephen Dedalus, "I have." "Pity is the feeling which arrests the mind in the presence of whatsoever is grave and constant in human sufferings and unites it with the human sufferer. Terror is the feeling which arrests the mind in the presence of whatsoever is grave and constant in human sufferings and unites it with the secret cause." Tragedy, then, seems to demand both the human sufferer and the secret cause: that is to say, the doubt, the pain, the pity of the human sufferer; and the affirmation, the awe, the terror of the secret cause. It is an affirmation even though the cause is destructive in its immediate effects: for this cause seems to affirm the existence of some universal order of things.

From this standpoint we can estimate the enormous problem that faces the modern writer in his quest for tragedy. For with Ibsen, as we have seen, this power of double vision is in some difficulty. In *Ghosts* or in *Rosmersholm* the element of affirmation is almost overwhelmed by the horror and the suffering that come from the operation of the secret cause—here represented by the family heritage—the dead husband, the dead wife. The affirmation is present, however, as Mr. Reichardt has pointed out, in the salvation of an individual's integrity. Ibsen's *Ghosts,* which has the rain pouring down outside for most of the play, nevertheless ends with a view of bright sunshine on

"The Unreferable Rain" (Editor's title). *From "The Saint as Tragic Hero" by Louis L. Martz, in* Tragic Themes in Western Literature, *ed. Cleanth Brooks (New Haven: Yale University Press, 1955), pp. 153–54. Copyright © 1955 by Yale University Press. Reprinted by permission of the author.*

the glaciers: symbolizing, perhaps, the clear self-realization which the heroine has achieved. But it is not a very long step before we exit— left—from these shattered drawing rooms into the rain of Ernest Hemingway, where we have the human sufferers, "alone and self-reliant," without a touch of any secret cause. We are in the world of pity which Santayana has beautifully described in a passage of his *Realms of Being*, where he speaks of the "unreasoning sentiment" he might feel in seeing a "blind old beggar" in a Spanish town: "pity simply, the pity of existence, suffusing, arresting, rendering visionary the spectacle of the moment and spreading blindly outwards, like a light in the dark, towards objects which it does not avail to render distinguishable."

It seems a perfect account of the central and powerful effect achieved in many of the best efforts of the modern stage, or movie, or novel, works of pity, where pity dissolves the scene, resolves it into the dew that Hamlet considers but transcends. Thus *A Farewell to Arms* is enveloped in symbolic rain; in *The Naked and the Dead* humanity is lost in the dim Pacific jungle; and the haze of madness gradually dissolves the realistic setting of *A Streetcar Named Desire* or *Death of a Salesman*. In the end, Willy Loman has to plant his garden in the dark. "The pity of existence . . . spreading blindly outwards . . . towards objects which it does not avail to render distinguishable."

Carlos Baker: The Mountain and the Plain

> "Learn about the human heart and the human mind in war from this book."—Hemingway, in another connection.[1]

Landscape in Gorizia

The opening chapter of Hemingway's second novel, *A Farewell to Arms,* is a generically rendered landscape with thousands of moving figures. It does much more than start the book. It helps to establish the dominant mood (which is one of doom), plants a series of important images for future symbolic cultivation, and subtly compels the reader into the position of detached observer.

"*The Mountain and the Plain*." *From* Hemingway: The Writer as Artist, *rev. ed., by Carlos Baker (Princeton: Princeton University Press, 1963), pp. 94–96, 101–8. Copyright © 1963 by Carlos Baker. Reprinted by permission of the publisher.*

[1] Hemingway, *Men at War*, introd., p. xx.

"In the late summer of that year we lived in a house in a village that looked across the river and the plain to the mountains. In the bed of the river there were pebbles and boulders, dry and white in the sun, and the water was clear and swiftly moving and blue in the channels. Troops went by the house and down the road and the dust they raised powdered the leaves of the trees. The trunks of the trees too were dusty and the leaves fell early that year and we saw the troops marching along the road and the dust rising and leaves, stirred by the breeze, falling and the soldiers marching and afterward the road bare and white, except for the leaves."

The first sentence here fixes the reader in a house in the village where he can take a long view across the river and the plain to the distant mountains. Although he does not realize it yet, the plain and the mountains (not to mention the river and the trees, the dust and the leaves) have a fundamental value as symbols. The autumnal tone of the language is important in establishing the autumnal mood of the chapter. The landscape itself has the further importance of serving as a general setting for the whole first part of the novel. Under these values, and of basic structural importance, are the elemental images which compose this remarkable introductory chapter.

The second sentence, which draws attention from the mountainous background to the bed of the river in the middle distance, produces a sense of clearness, dryness, whiteness, and sunninesss which is to grow very subtly under the artist's hands until it merges with one of the novel's two dominant symbols, the mountain-image. The other major symbol is the plain. Throughout the substructure of the book it is opposed to the mountain-image. Down this plain the river flows. Across it, on the dusty road among the trees, pass the men-at-war, faceless and voiceless and unidentified against the background of the spreading plain.

In the third and fourth sentences of this beautifully managed paragraph the march-past of troops and vehicles begins. From the reader's elevated vantage-point, looking down on the plain, the river, and the road, the continuously parading men are reduced in size and scale— made to seem smaller, more pitiful, more pathetic, more like wraiths blown down the wind, than would be true if the reader were brought close enough to overhear their conversation or see them as individualized personalities.

Between the first and fourth sentences, moreover, Hemingway accomplishes the transition from late summer to autumn—an inexorability of seasonal change which prepares the way for the study in doom on which he is embarked. Here again the natural elements take on a symbolic function. In the late summer we have the dust; in the early autumn the dust and the leaves falling; and through them both the marching troops impersonally seen. The reminder, through the dust, of the words of the funeral service in the prayer-book is fortified by the second natural symbol, the falling leaves. They dry out, fall, decay, and become part of the dust. Into the dust is where the troops are going—some of them soon, all of them eventually.

The short first chapter closes with winter, and the establishment of rain as a symbol of disaster. "At the start of the winter came the permanent rain and with the rain came the cholera. But it was checked and in the end only seven thousand died of it in the army." Already, now in the winter, seven thousand of the wraiths have vanished underground. The permanent rain lays the dust and rots the leaves as if they had never existed. There is no excellent beauty, even in the country around Gorizia, that has not some sadness to it. And there is hardly a natural beauty in the whole first chapter of *A Farewell to Arms* which has not some symbolic function in Hemingway's first study in doom. . . .

Home and Not-Home

As its first chapter suggests, the natural-mythological structure which informs *A Farewell to Arms* is in some ways comparable to the Burguete-Montparnasse, Catholic-Pagan, and Romero-Cohn contrasts of *The Sun Also Rises*. One has the impression, however, of greater assurance, subtlety, and complexity in the second novel, as if the writing of the first had strengthened and consolidated Hemingway's powers and given him new insights into this method for controlling materials from below.

Despite the insistent, denotative matter-of-factness at the surface of the presentation, the subsurface activity of *A Farewell to Arms* is organized connotatively around two poles. By a process of accrual and coagulation, the images tend to build round the opposed concepts of Home and Not-Home. Neither, of course, is truly conceptualistic; each is a kind of poetic intuition, charged with emotional values and woven, like a cable, of many strands. The Home-concept, for example, is associated with the mountains; with dry-cold weather; with peace and quiet; with love, dignity, health, happiness, and the good life; and with worship or at least the consciousness of God. The Not-Home concept is associated with low-lying plains; with rain and fog; with obscenity, indignity, disease, suffering, nervousness, war and death; and with irreligion.

The motto of William Bird's Three Mountains Press in Paris, which printed Hemingway's *In Our Time,* was "Levavi oculos meos in montes." The line might also have served as an epigraph for *A Farewell to*

Arms. Merely introduced in the first sentence of the first chapter, the mountain-image begins to develop important associations as early as Chapter Two. Learning that Frederick Henry is to go on leave, the young priest urges him to visit Capracotta in the Abruzzi. "There," he says, "is good hunting. You would like the people and though it is cold, it is clear and dry. You could stay with my family. My father is a famous hunter." But the lowlander infantry captain interrupts: "Come on," he says in pidgin Italian to Frederick Henry. "We go whorehouse before it shuts." [2]

After Henry's return from the leave, during which he has been almost everywhere else on the Italian peninsula *except* Abruzzi, the mountain-image gets further backing from another low-land contrast. "I had wanted," says he, "to go to Abruzzi. I had gone to no place where the roads were frozen and hard as iron, where it was clear cold and dry and the snow was dry and powdery and haretracks in the snow and the peasants took off their hats and called you Lord and there was good hunting. I had gone to no such place but to the smoke of cafés and nights when the room whirled and you needed to look at the wall to make it stop, nights in bed, drunk, when you knew that that was all there was."

Throughout Book I, Hemingway quietly consolidates the mountain-image. On the way up towards the Isonzo from Gorizia, Frederick looks across the river and the plain to the Julian and Carnic Alps. "I looked to the north at the two ranges of mountains, green and dark to the snow-line and then white and lovely in the sun. Then, as the road mounted along the ridge, I saw a third range of mountains, higher snow mountains, that looked chalky white and furrowed, with strange planes, and then there were mountains far beyond all these that you could hardly tell if you really saw." [3] Like Pope in the celebrated "Alps on Alps arise" passage, Hemingway is using the mountains symbolically. Years later, in "The Snows of Kilimanjaro," he would use the mighty peak of East Africa as a natural image of immortality, just as in *The Green Hills of Africa* he would build his narrative in part upon a contrast between the hill-country and the Serengetti Plain. When Frederick Henry lowers his eyes from the far-off ranges, he sees the plain and the river, the war-making equipment, and "the broken houses of the little town" which is to be occupied, if anything is left of it to occupy, during the coming attack. Already now, a few dozen pages into the book, the mountain-image has developed associations; with the man of God and his homeland, with clear dry cold and snow, with polite and kindly people, with hospitality,

[2] *FTA*, pp. 9, 13.
[3] *FTA*, p. 48.

and with natural beauty. Already it has its oppositions: the lowland obscenities of the priest-baiting captain, cheap cafés, one-night prostitutes, drunkenness, destruction, and the war.

When the trench-mortar explosion nearly kills Henry, the priest comes to visit him in the field-hospital, and the Abruzzi homeland acquires a religious association. "There in my country," says the priest, it is understood that a man may love God. It is not a dirty joke." Repeating, for emphasis, the effect of the priest's first account of the highland country, Hemingway allows Frederick to develop in his mind's eye an idyllic picture of the priest's home-ground.

"At Capracotta, he had told me, there were trout in the stream below the town. It was forbidden to play the flute at night . . . because it was bad for the girls to hear. . . . Aquila was a fine town. It was cool in the summer at night and the spring in Abruzzi was the most beautiful in Italy. But what was lovely was the fall to go hunting through the chestnut woods. The birds were all good because they fed on grapes, and you never took a lunch because the peasants were always honored if you would eat with them in their houses. . . ." [4]

By the close of Book I, largely through the agency of the priest, a complex connection has come clear between the idea of Home and the combination of high ground, cold weather, love, and the love of God. Throughout, Hemingway has worked solely by suggestion, implication, and quiet repetition, putting the reader into potential awareness, readying him for what is to come.

The next step is to bring Catherine Barkley by degrees into the center of the image. Her love affair with Henry begins as a "rotten game" of war-time seduction. Still emotionally unstable and at loose nervous ends from her fiancé's death, Catherine is a comparatively easy conquest. But in the American hospital at Milan, following Henry's ordeal by fire at the front not far from the Isonzo, the casual affair becomes an honorable though unpriested marriage. Because she can make a "home" of any room she occupies—and Henry several times alludes to this power of hers—Catherine naturally moves into association with ideas of home, love, and happiness. She does not really reach the center of the mountain-image until, on the heels of Frederick's harrowing lowland experiences during the retreat from Caporetto, the lovers move to Switzerland. Catherine is the first to go, and Henry follows her there as if she were the genius of the mountains, beckoning him on. Soon they are settled into a supremely happy life in the winterland on the mountainside above Montreux. Catherine's death occurs at Lausanne, after the March rains and the approaching need for a good lying-in hospital have driven the young couple down from their magic mountain—the closest approximation

[4] *FTA,* p. 78.

to the priest's fair homeland in the Abruzzi that they are ever to know. The total structure of the novel is developed, in fact, around the series of contrasting situations already outlined. To Gorizia, the Not-Home of war, succeeds the Home which Catherine and Frederick make together in the Milan Hospital. The Not-Home of the grim retreat from the Isonzo is followed by the quiet and happy retreat which the lovers share above Montreux. Home ends for Frederick Henry when he leaves Catherine dead in the Lausanne Hospital.

Developed for an esthetic purpose, Hemingway's contrasting images have also a moral value. Although he has nothing to say about the images themselves, Mr. Ludwig Lewisohn is undoubtedly correct in saying that *A Farewell to Arms* "proves once again the ultimate identity of the moral and the esthetic." In this critic's view, Hemingway "transcended the moral nihilism of the school he had himself helped to form" by the very intensity of his feelings for the contrast of love and war. "The simply wrought fable," Lewisohn continues, ignoring all the symbolic complexities yet still making a just appraisal, "has two culminations—the laconic and terrible one in which the activity of the battle police brings to an end the epically delineated retreat of the Italian army with its classically curbed rage and pity . . . and that other and final culmination in Switzerland with its blending in so simple and moving a fashion of the eternal notes of love and death." The operation of the underlying imagery, once its purposes are understood, doubly underscores Mr. Lewisohn's point that there is no moral nihilism in the central story of *A Farewell to Arms*.[5]

The use of rain as a kind of symbolic obligato in the novel has been widely and properly admired. Less apparent to the cursory reader is the way in which the whole idea of climate is related to the natural-mythological structure. (Hemingway's clusters of associated images produce emotional "climates" also, but they are better experienced than reduced by critical descriptions.) The rains begin in Italy during October, just before Henry's return to Gorizia after his recovery from his wounds. The rains continue, at first steadily, then intermittently, throughout the disastrous retreat, Henry's flight to Stresa, and the time of his reunion with Catherine. When they awaken the morning after their reunion night, the rain has stopped, light floods the window, and Henry, looking out in the fresh early morning, can see Lake Maggiore in the sun "with the mountains beyond." Towards these mountains the lovers now depart.

Not until they are settled in idyllic hibernation in their rented chalet above Montreux are they really out of the rain. As if to emphasize by climatic accompaniment their "confused alarums of struggle

[5] *Expression in America*, New York, 1932, p. 519.

and flight," the rain has swept over them during their escape up the lake in an open boat. Once in the mountains, however, they are out of the lowlands, out of danger, out of the huge, tired debacle of the war. Above Montreux, as in the priest's homeland of Abruzzi, the ridges are "iron-hard with the frost." The deep snow isolates them, and gives them a feeling of domestic safety, tranquillity, and invulnerability.

For several months the rainless idyll continues. "We lived through the months of January and February and the winter was very fine and we were very happy. There had been short thaws when the wind blew warm and the snow softened and the air felt like spring, but always the clear, hard cold had come again and the winter had returned. In March came the first break in the winter. In the night it started raining."

The reader has been prepared to recognize some kind of disaster-symbol in the return of the rains. Much as in *Romeo and Juliet,* several earlier premonitions of doom have been inserted at intervals. "I'm afraid of the rain," says Catherine in the Milan Hospital one summer night, "because sometimes I see me dead in it." In the fall, just before Henry returns to the front, they are in a Milan hotel. During a break in the conversation the sound of falling rain comes in. A motor car klaxons, and Henry quotes Marvell: "At my back I always hear Time's wingèd chariot hurrying near." He must soon take a cab to catch the train that will project him, though he does not know it yet, into the disaster of the great retreat. Months later, in Lausanne, the Marvell lines echo hollowly: "We knew the baby was very close now and it gave us both a feeling *as though something were hurrying us and we could not lose any time together.*" (Italics added.) The sound of the rain continues like an undersong until, with Catherine dead in the hospital room (not unlike that other happy one where their child was conceived), Henry walks back to the hotel in the rain.[6]

One further reinforcement of the central symbolic structure is provided by the contrast between the priest and the doctor, the man of God and the man without God. In line with the reminiscence of *Romeo and Juliet,* it may not be fantastic to see them respectively as the Friar Lawrence and the Mercutio of Hemingway's novel. The marked contrast between the two men becomes especially apparent when Henry returns to the Gorizia area following his discharge from the hospital.

The return to Gorizia is a sharp come-down. After the "home-feel-

---

[6] *FTA*, pp. 135, 165, 267, 326, and 332 show, in order, the various premonitions and the obligato use of rain. Malcolm Cowley was one of the first of Hemingway's critics to point to his symbolic use of weather. See *The Portable Hemingway,* New York, 1944, introd., p. xvi.

ing" of the hospital and the hotel in Milan, the old army post seems
less like home than ever. The tenor of life there has noticeably
changed. A kind of damp-rot afflicts morale. The major, bringing
Henry up to date on the state of affairs, plays dismally on the word
bad. It has been a "bad summer." It was "very bad" on the Bainsizza
plateau: "We lost three cars. . . . You wouldn't believe how bad it's
been. . . . You were lucky to be hit when you were. . . . Next year
will be worse. . . ." As if he were not fully convinced by the Major's
despair, Henry picks up the word: "Is it so bad?" The answer is yes.
"It is so bad and worse. Go get cleaned up and find your friend
Rinaldi."

With Rinaldi the doctor, things also are bad, a fact which has been
borne in upon the major so strongly that he thinks of Rinaldi when he
mentions the word *bad*. Things are not bad for Rinaldi from a professional point of view, for he has operated on so many casualties that
he has become "a lovely surgeon." Still, he is not the old Mercutio-
like and mercurial Rinaldi. If mercury enters into his picture at all
it is because he has syphilis, or thinks he has. He is treating himself
for it and is beginning to entertain certain delusions of persecution.
Except for his work, and the temporary opiates of drink and prostitutes, both of which interfere with his work, Rinaldi, the man of
the plain, the man without God, is a man without resources.

With the priest, the man from the Abruzzi highlands, tacitly rein-
troduced as a contrast for Rinaldi, things are not so bad. "He was
the same as ever," says Henry at their meeting, "small and brown
and compact-looking." He is much more sure of himself than formerly, though in a modest way. When Rinaldi, in the absence of the
foul-mouthed captain, takes up the former indoor game of priest-
baiting, the priest is not perturbed. "I could see," says Henry, "that
the baiting did not touch him now."

Out of the evils of the past summer the priest has even contrived
to gather a nascent hope. Officers and men, he thinks, are gentling
down because they "realize the war" as never before. When this happens, the fighting cannot continue for very much longer. Henry, playing half-heartedly the *advocatus diaboli,* argues that what the priest
calls "gentling down" is really nothing but the feeling of defeat: "It
is in defeat that we become Christian . . . like Our Lord." Henry
is maintaining that after the fearless courage of His ministry, Our
Lord's gentleness and His refusal to fight against the full brunt of
the experience on Calvary became the ideal of Christian meekness. If
Peter had rescued Christ Jesus from the Garden, suggests Henry,
Christian ethics might be something different. But the priest, who is
as compact as he looks, knows otherwise. Our Lord would not have
changed in any way. From that knowledge and belief comes the priest's

own strength. He has resources which Dr. Rinaldi, the man without God, does not possess.[7]

The priest-doctor contrast is carried out in the sacred-versus-profane-love antithesis which is quietly emphasized in the novel. Through the agency of Rinaldi the love affair begins at a fairly low level. The doctor introduces Frederick to Catherine, and takes a jocularly profane view of the early infatuation, seeming to doubt that it can ever be anything but an unvarnished war-time seduction. On the other hand, the background symbols of home and true love and high ground suggest that the lovers' idyllic life in Switzerland is carried on under the spiritual aegis of the priest. Neither Rinaldi nor the priest appears in the latter part of the book. But when, having been driven to the lowlands by the rains of spring, Catherine enters the hospital, it is naturally enough a doctor who takes over. And though this doctor does all he can to save her life, Catherine dies.

Projected in actualistic terms and a matter-of-fact tone, telling the truth about the effects of war in human life, *A Farewell to Arms* is entirely and even exclusively acceptable as a naturalistic narrative of what happened. To read it only as such, however, is to miss the controlling symbolism: the deep central antithesis between the image of life and home (the mountain) and the image of war and death (the plain).

[7] On the low morale among the Italian troops, see *FTA*, pp. 174–75. On Rinaldi's affliction, see p. 181. On the priest's firmness, see pp. 183–84.

E. M. Halliday: Hemingway's Ambiguity: Symbolism and Irony

There is, of course, a larger sense, germane to all good fiction, in which Hemingway may be said to be symbolic in his narrative method: the sense which indicates his typical creation of key characters who are representative on several levels. We thus find Jake Barnes's war-wound impotence a kind of metaphor for the whole atmosphere of sterility and frustration which is the *ambiance* of *The Sun Also Rises;* we find Catherine Barkley's naïve simplicity and warmth the right epitome for the idea and ideal of normal civilian home life to which Frederic Henry deserts; we find the old Cuban fisherman in some way representative of the whole human race in its natural struggle for survival. But the recent criticism of Hemingway as symbolist goes far

"Hemingway's Ambiguity: Symbolism and Irony" by *E. M. Halliday.* From American Literature 27 (1956): 57–63. Copyright © 1956 by the Duke University Press. Reprinted by permission of the author and Duke University Press.

beyond such palpable observations as these, and in considering the fundamental character of his narrative technique I wish to turn attention to more ingenious if not esoteric explications.

Professor Carlos Baker, in *Hemingway: The Writer as Artist* (1952), has established himself as the leading oracle of Hemingway's symbolism. His book is, I think, the most valuable piece of extended Hemingway criticism that we yet have, and to a large extent its contribution is one of new insights into the symbolist aspect of his subject's narrative method. He is sweeping:

> From the first Hemingway has been dedicated as a writer to the rendering of *Wahrheit*, the precise and at least partly naturalistic rendering of things as they are and were. Yet under all his brilliant surfaces lies the controlling *Dichtung*, the symbolic underpainting which gives so remarkable a sense of depth and vitality to what otherwise might be flat two-dimensional portraiture.[1]

This may fairly be said to represent Mr. Baker's major thesis, and he develops and supports it with remarkable energy and skill. I do not wish to disparage his over-all effort—he is often very enlightening— but I do wish to argue that he has been rather carried away by his thesis, and that therein he eminently typifies the new symbolist criticism of Hemingway which in its enthusiasm slights or ignores other basic aspects of Hemingway's technique.

Mr. Baker's chapter on *A Farewell to Arms* is an original piece of criticism, and it solidly illustrates his approach. He finds that the essential meaning of this novel is conveyed by two master symbols, the Mountain and the Plain, which organize the *Dichtung* around "two poles":

> By a process of accrual and coagulation, the images tend to build round the opposed concepts of Home and Not-Home. . . . The Home-concept, for example, is associated with the mountains; with dry-cold weather; with peace and quiet; with love, dignity, health, happiness, and the good life; and with worship or at least the consciousness of God. The Not-Home concept is associated with low-lying plains; with rain and fog; with obscenity, indignity, disease, suffering, nervousness, war and death; and with irreligion.[2]

It is in terms of these antipodal concepts that Mr. Baker analyzes the semantic structure of *A Farewell to Arms*, a structure which he finds effective chiefly because of the adroit and subtle development of the correspondingly antipodal symbols, the Mountain and the Plain. He

---

[1] Carlos Baker, *Hemingway: The Writer as Artist* (Princeton: Princeton University Press, 1952), p. 289.

[2] *Ibid.*, pp. 101, 102.

argues that from the first page of the story these are set up in their signficant antithesis, that they are the key to the relationships among several of the leading characters, and that the central action—Frederic Henry's desertion from the Italian Army to join Catherine Barkley, the British nurse—can be fully appreciated only on this symbolic basis. "*A Farewell to Arms*," he concludes, "is entirely and even exclusively acceptable as a naturalistic narrative of what happened. To read it only as such, however, is to miss the controlling symbolism: the deep central antithesis between the image of life and home (the mountain) and the image of war and death (the plain)." [3]

Clearly there is some truth in this. The "deep central antithesis" cannot be denied, I would think, by anyone with an acceptable understanding of the book. The question at issue is one of technique; to what extent, and how precisely, is the central antithesis in fact engineered around the Mountain and the Plain as symbols?

One thing is noticeable immediately: as in virtually all of Hemingway, anything that can possibly be construed to operate symbolically does no violence whatsoever to the naturalism (or realism) of the story on the primary level. Nothing could be a more natural—or more traditional—symbol of purity, of escape from the commonplace, in short of elevation, than mountains. If thousands of people have read the passages in *A Farewell to Arms* which associate the mountains "with dry-cold weather; with peace and quiet; with love, dignity, health, happiness and the good life" without taking them to be "symbolic" it is presumably because these associations are almost second nature for all of us. Certainly this seems to be true of Frederic Henry: it is most doubtful that in the course of the novel he is ever to be imagined as consciously regarding the mountains as a symbol. This of course does not prove that Hemingway did not regard them as such, or that the full understanding of this novel as an art structure does not perhaps require the symbolic equation, *mountain* equals *life and home*. It does, however, point differentially to another type of symbolism, where the character in question is shown to be clearly aware of the trope, as when Catherine Barkley says she hates rain because "sometimes I see me dead in it," [4] or when Frederic Henry says of his plunge into the Tagliamento, "Anger was washed away in the river along with any obligation." [5]

But Mr. Baker has claimed a most exact and detailed use by Hemingway of the Mountain-Plain symbolism, and his ingenious interpretation deserves closer attention. Like many other critics he is an intense

[3] *Ibid.*, pp. 108, 109.
[4] *A Farewell to Arms*, p. 135.
[5] *Ibid.*, p. 248.

admirer of the novel's opening paragraph, which, he says, "does much more than start the book. It helps to establish the dominant mood (which is one of doom), plants a series of important images for future symbolic cultivation, and subtly compels the reader into the position of detached observer." [6] He proceeds to a close analysis of this paragraph:

> The second sentence, which draws attention from the mountainous background to the bed of the river in the middle distance, produces a sense of clearness, dryness, whiteness, and sunniness which is to grow very subtly under the artist's hands until it merges with one of the novel's two dominant symbols, the mountain-image. The other major symbol is the plain. Throughout the sub-structure of the book it is opposed to the mountain-image. Down this plain the river flows. Across it, on the dusty road among the trees, pass the men-at-war, faceless and voiceless and unidentified against the background of the spreading plain.[7]

This is highly specific, and we are entitled to examine it minutely. Mr. Baker says the river is "in the middle distance" in the direction of the mountains with the image of which, as he sees it, the symbolic images of the river are to merge into one great symbol. But is the river really in the middle distance? The narrator tells us he can see not only its boulders but its pebbles, "dry and white in the sun." The river must, of course, flow from the mountains, but in the perspective seen from the house occupied by Frederic Henry, it would appear to be very close at hand—closer than the plain, and quite in contrast to the distant mountains. And this raises the question of whether the clearness, dryness, whiteness, and sunniness offered by the river are in fact artfully intended to be associated with the mountain-image and what it is held to symbolize; or, disregarding the question of intent, whether they do in fact so operate in the artistic structure. Why must the river images be disassociated from the images of the plain across which the river, naturally, flows? Because the river images are of a kind which, if they work as symbols, are incongruent with what Mr. Baker has decided the Plain stands for; they must instead be allocated to the Mountain. This is so important to his thesis that the river shifts gracefully, but without textual support, into "the middle distance," closer to the mountains.

And what of the soldiers on the road? Since they must be firmly associated with the Plain ("war and death"), it is against that background that Mr. Baker sees them in Hemingway's opening paragraph —it would not do to see them against the background of the river, with its Mountain images. But let us look again at the paragraph.

[6] Baker, *op. cit.*, p. 94.
[7] *Ibid.*, pp. 94–95.

In the late summer of that year we lived in a house in a village that looked across the river and the plain to the mountains. In the bed of the river there were pebbles and boulders, dry and white in the sun, and the water was clear and swiftly moving and blue in the channels. Troops went by the house and down the road and the dust they raised powdered the leaves of the trees.

Mr. Baker says the road is across the river, as of course it would have to be if we are to see the figures of the soldiers against the background of the plain. Hemingway does not say the road is across the river. Indeed, everything indicates the opposite arrangement: a house on a road running along the near side of the river, across which the plain stretches out to the mountains. "Sometimes in the dark," begins the third paragraph of the novel, "we heard the troops marching under the window. . . ."

The truth is that a strong part of Mr. Baker's initially persuasive exegesis of the opening paragraph of *A Farewell to Arms* hangs on a reading that the written words will not support. This is not to deny that the paragraph establishes a mood of doom by its somber tone and the epitomic symbols of dust and falling leaves: what I am questioning is the over-all symbolic organization of the novel's structure in terms of the Mountain and the Plain, which Mr. Baker argues as a prime illustration of his unequivocal judgment of Hemingway as symbolist artist.

As a matter of fact, the plain presented in the opening pages of *A Farewell to Arms* is as troublesome as the river when it comes to supporting Mr. Baker's interpretation. There are plains in many countries that could well serve as symbols of emptiness, desolation, disaster, and death—we have some in the American West. But this does not appear to be that sort of plain: quite the contrary. "The plain," Frederic Henry narrates in the opening words of the second paragraph, "was rich with crops; there were many orchards of fruit trees. . . ." Mr. Baker tells us neither how these images of fertility and fruition are to fit in with "rain and fog; with obscenity, indignity, disease, suffering, nervousness, war and death," nor how we should symbolically interpret the conclusion of the sentence, ". . . and beyond the plain the mountains were brown and bare." One can easily grant that as the novel unfolds, the impression of war itself grows steadily more saturated with a sense of doomsday qualities: that was an essential part of Hemingway's theme. But to what degree is this impression heightened by the use of the Plain as symbol? The simple exigencies of history prevent exclusive association of the war with the plain as opposed to the mountains, as the narrator indicates on the first page: "There was fighting in the mountains and at night we could see flashes from the artillery." Yet if Mr. Baker is right we would expect to find, despite this difficulty, a salient artistic emphasis of the Plain in symbolic association with all those images which his interpretation sets against those coalescing around the Mountain symbol.

Mr. Baker makes much of the fact that Frederic Henry, during his leave, fails to take advantage of the offer of his friend the chaplain and go to the high mountain country of the Abruzzi, "where the roads were frozen and hard as iron, where it was clear cold and dry and the snow was dry and powdery. . . . I had gone to no such place but to the smoke of cafés and nights when the room whirled and you needed to look at the wall to make it stop, nights in bed, drunk, when you knew that that was all there was." [8] Here, Mr. Baker claims, "the mountain-image gets further backing from another lowland contrast." [9] Granting the familiar association here of mountain-country with certain delectable and longed-for experiences, one would like to see, in support of the Mountain-Plain explication, a clearer identification of the contrasting, soldier-on-leave experiences, with the lowland or plain. And while wondering about this, one reads on in *A Farewell to Arms* and soon finds Frederic Henry and Catherine Barkley in Milan, where Henry is recuperating from his wound. They are having a wonderful time. They are in love, have frequent opportunities to be alone together in the hospital room, go often to the races, dine at the town's best restaurants, and in general lead an existence that makes the most pleasant contrast imaginable to the dismal life at the front. "We had a lovely time that summer," [10] says the hero. What has happened here to the Mountain-Plain machinery? It does not seem to be operating; or perhaps it is operating in reverse, since Milan is definitely in the plain. Mr. Baker passes over these pages of the novel rather quickly, remarking that Catherine here "moves into association with ideas of home, love and happiness." [11] He seems to be aware of the difficulty, although he does not mention it as such: "She does not really [sic] reach the center of the mountain-image until, on the heels of Frederic's harrowing lowland experiences during the retreat from Caporetto, the lovers move to Switzerland. Catherine is the first to go, and Henry follows her there as if she were the genius of the mountains, beckoning him on." [12]

This is romantically pleasant, but inaccurate. Catherine does not go to Switzerland, but to the Italian resort village of Stresa, on Lake Maggiore. Stresa, moreover, although surrounded by mountains, is

[8] *A Farewell to Arms*, p. 13.
[9] Baker, *op. cit.*, p. 102.
[10] *A Farewell to Arms*, p. 119.
[11] Baker, *op. cit.*, p. 104.
[12] *Ibid.*

itself distinctly lowland: you can pedal a bicycle from Milan or Turin without leaving nearly flat country. Still, it can be allowed that the lovers are not free of the contaminating shadow of war until they have escaped up the lake to Switzerland and established themselves in their little chalet above Montreux. Here, again, the associations all of us are likely to make with high-mountain living assert themselves—clear, cold air; magnificent views; white snow; peace and quiet—and the hero and heroine are shown to be happily aware of these. The rain, however, which they have both come to regard as an omen of disaster, grants no immunity to the mountain; it refuses to preserve a unilateral symbolic association with the plain. Mr. Baker knows this, but does not discuss the extent to which it obscures his neat Mountain-Plain antithesis, making the point instead that "the March rains and the approaching need for a good lying-in hospital have driven the young couple down from their magic mountain" to "the lowlands" [13] of Lausanne. Here again observation is fuzzy to the point of distortion: Lausanne happens to stand on a series of steep hills and is an extraordinarily poor specimen of a City of the Plain. This is clear, incidentally, without reference to an atlas, since there are several allusions to the hills and steep streets of Lausanne in the novel itself.[14] But Mr. Baker is caught up in his symbolic apparatus, and if one symbol of death (rain) has failed to stay where it belongs in his scheme (on the plain) he still is persuaded to see the topography of Switzerland in a light that will not darken his thesis.

What all this illustrates, it seems to me, is that Mr. Baker has allowed an excellent insight into Hemingway's imagery and acute sense of natural metonymy to turn into an interesting but greatly over-elaborated critical gimmick. It is undeniable that in the midst of the darkling plain of struggle and flight which was the war in Italy, Frederic Henry thinks of the Swiss Alps as a neutral refuge of peace and happiness—surely millions must have lifted their eyes to those mountains with like thoughts during both World Wars. But in so far as this is symbolism it belongs to our race and culture; and if it is to be sophisticated into a precise scheme of artistic implication revolving around two distinct polar symbols, the signals transmitted from artist to reader must be more clearly semaphored than anything Mr. Baker has been able to point to accurately. I do not believe this is derogatory to Hemingway. Sensitive as always to those parts of experience that are suggestive and connotative, he used the mountain metaphor which is part of our figurative heritage to deepen the thematic contrast in *A Farewell to Arms,* between war and not-war. But no-

[13] *Ibid.*, pp. 104, 108.
[14] See, for instance, pp. 328, 331, 334.

where did he violate realism for the sake of this metaphor; nor did he, as I read the novel, set up the artificially rigid and unrealistic contrast between the Mountain and the Plain which Mr. Baker's analysis requires.

Mr. Baker himself has summed up the sequel to his investigation of *A Farewell to Arms*. "Once the reader has become aware of what Hemingway is doing in those parts of his work which lie below the surface, he is likely to find symbols operating everywhere. . . ." [15] Mr. Baker does find them everywhere, and they not infrequently trip him into strangely vulnerable judgments. Finding an unprecedented display of symbolism in *Across the River and Into the Trees* (1950), for instance, he is willing to accord that disappointing novel a richly favorable verdict: "a prose poem, with a remarkably complex emotional structure, on the theme of the three ages of man. . . . If *A Farewell to Arms* was his *Romeo and Juliet* . . . this . . . could perhaps be called a lesser kind of *Winter's Tale* or *Tempest*." [16]

[15] Baker, *op. cit.*, p. 117.
[16] *Ibid.*, pp. 264, 287.

The "Dumb Ox" in Love and War

by Wyndham Lewis

Ernest Hemingway is a very considerable artist in prose-fiction. Besides this, or with this, his work possesses a penetrating quality, like an animal speaking. Compared often with Hemingway, William Faulkner is an excellent, big-strong, novelist: but a conscious artist he cannot be said to be. Artists are made, not born: but he is considerably older, I believe, than Hemingway, so it is not that. But my motive for discussing these two novelists has not been to arrive at estimates of that sort.

A quality in the work of the author of *Men Without Women* suggests that we are in the presence of a writer who is not merely a conspicuous chessman in the big-business book-game of the moment, but something much finer than that. Let me attempt to isolate that quality for you, in such a way as not to damage it too much: for having set out to demonstrate the political significance of this artist's work, I shall, in the course of that demonstration, resort to a dissection of it—not the best way, I am afraid, to bring out the beauties of the finished product. This dissection is, however, necessary for my purpose here. "I have a weakness for Ernest Hemingway," as the egregious Miss Stein says:[1] it is not agreeable to me to pry into his craft, but there is no help for it if I am to reach certain important conclusions.

But *political significance!* That is surely the last thing one would expect to find in such books as *In Our Time, The Sun also Rises, Men Without Women,* or *Farewell to Arms*. And indeed it is difficult to imagine a writer whose mind is more entirely closed to politics than is Hemingway's. I do not suppose he has ever heard of the Five-Year Plan, though I dare say he knows that artists pay no income tax in Mexico, and is quite likely to be following closely the agitation of the Mexican matadors to get themselves recognized as 'artists' so that they may pay no income tax. I expect he has heard of Hitler, but thinks

"The Dumb Ox in Love and War" (original title: *"The Dumb Ox"*). From Men Without Art by *Wyndham Lewis* (*New York: Russell & Russell, 1964*), *pp. 17–41. Copyright © 1934 by Wyndham Lewis. Reprinted by permission of the publisher.*

[1] *The Autobiography of Alice B. Toklas.*

of him mainly, if he is acquainted with the story, as the Boche who went down into a cellar with another Boche and captured thirty Frogs and came back with an Iron Cross. He probably knows that his friend Pound writes a good many letters every week to American papers on the subject of Social Credit, but I am sure Pound has never succeeded in making him read a line of *Credit-Power and Democracy*. He is interested in the sports of death, in the sad things that happen to those engaged in the sports of love—in sand-sharks and in Wilson-spoons—in war, but *not* in the things that cause war, or the people who profit by it, or in the ultimate human destinies involved in it. He lives, or affects to live, *submerged*. He is in the multitudinous ranks of *those to whom things happen*—terrible things of course, and of course stoically borne. He has never heard, or affects never to have heard, that there is another and superior element, inhabited by a type of unnatural men which preys upon that of the submerged type. Or perhaps it is not quite a submerged mankind to which he belongs, or affects to belong, but to something of the sort described in one of Faulkner's war stories: "But after twelve years," Faulkner writes, "I think of us as bugs in the surface of the water, isolant and aimless and unflagging. Not on the surface; in it, within that line of demarcation not air and not water, sometimes submerged, sometimes not." [2] (What a stupid and unpleasant word "isolant" is! Hemingway would be incapable of using such a word.) But—twelve, fifteen years afterwards—to be *submerged*, most of the time, is Hemingway's idea. It is a little bit of an *art pur* notion, but it is, I think, extremely effective, in his case. Faulkner is much less preoccupied with art for its own sake, and although he has obtained his best successes by submerging himself again (in an intoxicating and hysterical fluid) he does not like being submerged quite as well as Hemingway, and dives rather because he is compelled to dive by public opinion, I imagine, than because he feels at home in the stupid medium of the sub-world, the bêtise of the herd. Hemingway has really taken up his quarters there, and has mastered the medium entirely, so that he is of it and yet not of it in a very satisfactory way.

Another manner of looking at it would be to say that Ernest Hemingway is the Noble Savage of Rousseau, but a white version, the simple American man. That is at all events the rôle that he has chosen, and he plays it with an imperturbable art and grace beyond praise.

It is not perhaps necessary to say that Hemingway's art is an art of the surface—and, as I look at it, none the worse for that. It is almost purely an art of action, and of very violent action, which is another qualification. Faulkner's is that too: but violence with Hemingway is deadly matter-of-fact (as if there were only violent action and nothing

[2] *Ad Astra*. William Faulkner.

else in the world): whereas with Faulkner it is an excited crescendo of psychological working-up of a sluggish and not ungentle universe, where there *might* be something else than high-explosive—if it were given a Chinaman's chance, which it is not. The latter is a far less artistic purveyor of violence. He does it well: but as to the manner, he does it in a way that any fool could do it. Hemingway, on the other hand, serves it up like the master of this form of art that he is, immeasurably more effective than Faulkner—good as he is; or than say the Irish novelist O'Flagherty—who is a *raffiné* too, or rather a two-gun man; Hemingway really banishes melodrama (except for his absurd escapes, on a Hollywood pattern, in *Farewell to Arms*).

To find a parallel to *In Our Time* or *Farewell to Arms* you have to go to *Colomba* or to *Chronique du règne de Charles ix*: and in one sense Prosper Merimée supplies the historical key to these two ex-soldiers—married, in their literary craft, to a theatre of action *a l'outrance*. The scenes at the siege of La Rochelle in the *Chronique du règne de Charles ix* for instance: in the burning of the mill when the ensign is roasted in the window, that is the Hemingway subjects-matter to perfection—a man melted in his armour like a shell-fish in its shell—melted lobster in its red armour.

S'ils tentaient de sauter par les fenêtres, ils tombaient dans les flammes, ou bien étaient reçus sur la pointe des piques. . . . Un enseigne, revêtu d'une armure complète, essaya de sauter comme les autres par une fenêtre étroite. Sa cuirasse se terminait, suivant une mode alors assez commune, par une espèce de jupon en fer qui couvrait les cuisses et le ventre, et s'élargissait comme le haut d'un entonnoir, de manière à permettre de marcher facilement. La fenêtre n'était pas assez large pour laisser passer cette partie de son armure, et l'enseigne, dans son trouble, s'y était précipité avec tant de violence, qu'il se trouva avoir la plus grande partie du corps en dehors sans pouvoir remuer, et pris comme dans un étau. Cependant les flammes montaient jusqu'à lui, échauffaient son armure, et l'y brûlaient lentement comme dans une fournaise ou dans ce fameux taureau d'airain inventé par Phalaris.[3]

Compare this with the following:

We were in a garden at Mons. Young Buckley came in with his patrol from across the river. The first German I saw climbed up over the garden wall. We waited till he got one leg over and then potted him. He had so much equipment on and looked awfully surprised and fell down into the garden. Then three more came over further down the wall. We shot them. They all came just like that.[4]

[3] *Chronique du règne de Charles ix*. Merimée.
[4] *In Our Time*. Hemingway.

"In no century would Prosper Merimée have been a theologian or metaphysician," and if that is true of Merimée, it is at least equally true of his American prototype. But their 'formulas' sound rather the same, "indifferent in politics . . . all the while he is feeding all his scholarly curiosity, his imagination, the very eye, with the, to him ever delightful, relieving, reassuring spectacle, of those straightforward forces in human nature, which are also matters of fact. There is the formula of Merimée! the enthusiastic amateur of rude, crude, naked force in men and women wherever it could be found . . . there are no half-lights . . . Sylla, the false Demetrius, Carmen, Colomba, that impassioned self within himself, have no atmosphere. Painfully distinct in outline, inevitable to sight, unrelieved, there they stand, like solitary mountain forms on some hard, perfectly transparent day. What Merimée gets around his singularly sculpturesque creations is neither more nor less than empty space." [5]

I have quoted the whole of this passage because it gives you "the formula," equally for the author of *Carmen* and of *The Sun Also Rises* —namely *the enthusiastic amateur of rude, crude, naked force in men and women:* but it also brings out very well, subsequently, the nature of the radical and extremely significant *difference* existing between these two men, of differing nations and epochs—sharing so singularly a taste for physical violence and for fine writing, but nothing else. Between them there is this deep gulf fixed: that gifted he of today is "the man that things are done to"—even the "I" in *The Sun Also Rises* allows his Jew puppet to knock him about and "put him to sleep" with a crash on the jaw, and this first person singular covers a very aimless, will-less person, to say the least of it: whereas that *he* of the world of *Carmen* (so much admired by Nietzsche for its bright Latin violence and directness—*la gaya scienza*) or of Corsican vendetta, he was in love with *will*, as much as with violence: he did not celebrate in his stories a spirit that suffered bodily injury and mental disaster with the stoicism of an athletic clown in a particularly brutal circus—or of oxen (however robust) beneath a crushing yoke: *he,* the inventor of Colomba, belonged to a race of men for whom action meant *their* acting, with all the weight and momentum of the whole of their being: *he* of post-Napoleonic France celebrated intense spiritual energy and purpose, using physical violence as a mere means to that only half-animal ideal. *Sylla, Demetrius, Colomba,* even *de Mergy,* summon to our mind a world bursting with purpose—even if always upon the personal and very animal plane, and with no more universal ends: while Hemingway's books, on the other hand, scarcely contain a figure who is not in some way futile, clown-like, passive, and above all *purposeless.* His world of men and women (*in violent action,* certainly) is completely empty of will. His puppets are leaves, *very vio-*

[5] *Miscellaneous Studies.* Walter Pater.

lently blown hither and thither; drugged or at least deeply intoxicated phantoms of a sort of matter-of-fact shell-shock.

In *Farewell to Arms* the hero is a young American who has come over to Europe for the fun of the thing, as an alternative to baseball, to take part in the Sport of Kings. It has not occurred to him that it is no longer the sport of kings, but the turning-point in the history of the earth at which he is assisting, when men must either cease thinking like children and abandon such sports, or else lose their freedom for ever, much more effectively than any mere *king* could ever cause them to lose it. For him, it remains "war" in the old-fashioned semi-sporting sense. Throughout this ghastly event, he proves himself a thorough-going sport, makes several hairbreadth, Fenimore Cooper-like, escapes, but never from first to last betrays a spark of intelligence. Indeed, his physical stoicism, admirable as it is, is as nothing to his really heroic imperviousness to thought. This "war"— Gallipoli, Paschendaele, Caporetto—is just another "scrap." The Anglo-Saxon American—the "Doughboy"—and the Anglo-Saxon Tommy—join hands, in fact, outrival each other in a stolid determination absolutely to ignore, come what may, what all this is about. Whoever may be in the secrets of destiny—may indeed be destiny itself—*they* are not nor ever will be. They are an integral part of that world *to whom things happen:* they are not those who cause or connive at the happenings, and that is perfectly clear.

> Pack up your troubles in your old kit bag,
> Smile boys, that's the style

and *keep smiling,* what's more, from ear to ear, a *should-I-worry?* "good sport" smile, as do the Hollywood Stars when they are being photographed, as did the poor Bairnsfather "Tommy"—the "muddied oaf at the goal"—of all oafishness!

I hope this does not seem irrelevant to you: it is not, let me reassure you, but very much the contrary. The roots of all these books are in the War of 1914–1918, as much those of Faulkner as those of Hemingway: it would be ridiculous of course to say that either of these two highly intelligent ex-soldiers shared the "oafish" mentality altogether: but the war-years were a democratic, a *levelling,* school, and both come from a pretty thoroughly "levelled" nation, where personality is the thing least liked. The rigid organization of the communal life as revealed in *Middletown,* for instance (or such a phenomenon as N.R.A.) is akin to the military state. So *will,* as expressed in the expansion of the individual, is not a thing we should expect to find illustrated by a deliberately typical American writer.

Those foci of passionate personal energy which we find in Merimée, we should look for in vain in the pages of Hemingway or Faulkner:

in place of Don José or of Colomba we get a pack of drugged or intoxicated marionettes. These differences are exceedingly important. But I shall be dealing with that more carefully in my next chapter. So any attempt to identify "the formula" for Prosper Merimée with that of Ernest Hemingway would break down. You are led at once to a realization of the critical difference between these two universes of discourse, both employing nothing but physical terms; of how an appetite for the extremity of violence exists in both, but in the one case it is personal ambition, family pride, romantic love that are at stake, and their satisfaction is violently sought and undertaken, whereas in the other case purposeless violence, for the sake of the "kick," is pursued and recorded, and the "thinking subject" is to regard himself as nothing more significant than a ripple beneath the breeze upon a pond.

If we come down to the manner, specifically to the style, in which these sensational impressions are conveyed, again most interesting discoveries await us: for, especially with Mr. Hemingway, the story is told in the tone, and with the vocabulary, of the persons described. The rhythm is the anonymous folk-rhythm of the urban proletariat. Mr. Hemingway is, self-consciously, a folk-prose-poet in the way that Robert Burns was a folk-poet. But what is curious about this is that the modified *Beach-la-mar* in which he writes, is, more or less, the speech that is proposed for everybody in the future—it is a volapuk which probably will be ours tomorrow. For if the chief executive of the United States greets the Roman Catholic democratic leader (Al Smith) with the exclamation "Hallo old potato!" today, the English political leaders will be doing so the day after tomorrow. And the Anglo-Saxon *Beach-la-mar* of the future will not be quite the same thing as Chaucer or Dante, contrasted with the learned tongue. For the latter was the speech of a race rather than of a class, whereas our "vulgar tongue" will really be *vulgar*.

But in the case of Hemingway the folk-business is very seriously complicated by a really surprising fact. He has suffered an overmastering influence, which cuts his work off from any other, except that of his mistress (for his master has been a *mistress!*). So much is this the case, that their destinies (his and that of the person who so strangely hypnotized him with her repeating habits and her *faux-naif* prattle) are for ever interlocked. His receptivity was so abnormally pronounced (even as a craftsman, this capacity for being *the person that things are done to* rather than the person who naturally initiates what is to be done to others, was so marked) and the affinity thus disclosed was found so powerful! I don't like speaking about this, for

it is such a first-class complication, and yet it is in a way so irrelevant
to the spirit which informs his work and must have informed it had
he never made this apparently overwhelming "contact." But there it
is: if you ask yourself how you would be able to tell a page of Hemingway, if it were unexpectedly placed before you, you would be compelled to answer, *Because it would be like Miss Stein!* And if you
were asked how you would know it was not by Miss Stein, you would
say, *Because it would probably be about prize-fighting, war, or the
bull-ring, and Miss Stein does not write about war, boxing or bull-
fighting!*

It is very uncomfortable in real life when people become so capti-
vated with somebody else's tricks that they become a sort of caricature
or echo of the other: and it is no less embarrassing in books, at least
when one entertains any respect for the victim of the fascination. But
let us take a passage or two and get this over—it is very unpleasant.
Let us take Krebs—the "he" in this passage is Krebs, a returned soldier in a Hemingway story:

> When he was in town their appeal to him was not very strong. He
> did not like them when he saw them in the Greek's ice-cream parlor.
> He did not want them themselves really. They were too complicated.
> There was something else. Vaguely he wanted a girl but he did not want
> to have to work to get her. He would have liked to have a girl but he
> did not want to have to spend a long time getting her. He did not want
> to get into the intrigue and the politics. He did not want to have to do
> any courting. He did not want to tell any more lies. It wasn't worth it.
>
> He did not want any consequences. He did not want any consequences
> ever again. He wanted to live along without consequences. Besides he did
> not really need a girl. The army had taught him that. It was all right to
> pose as though you had to have a girl. Nearly everybody did that. But it
> wasn't true. You did not need a girl. That was the funny thing. First a
> fellow boasted how girls mean nothing to him, that he never thought of
> them, that they could not touch him. Then a fellow boasted that he
> could not get along without girls, that he had to have them all the
> time, that he could not go to sleep without them.
>
> That was all a lie. It was all a lie both ways. You did not need a girl
> unless you thought about them. He learned that in the army. Then
> sooner or later you always got one. When you were really ripe for a girl
> you always got one. You did not have to think about it. Sooner or later
> it would come. He had learned that in the army.
>
> Now he would have liked a girl if she had come to him and not wanted
> to talk. But here at home it was all too complicated. He knew he could
> never get through it all again. It was not worth the trouble. That was
> the thing about French girls and German girls. There was not all this
> talking. You couldn't talk much and you did not need to talk. It was
> simple and you were friends. He thought about France and then he
> began to think about Germany. On the whole he liked Germany better.

He did not want to leave Germany. He did not want to come home. Still, he had come home. He sat on the front porch.

He liked the girls that were walking along the other side of the street. He liked the look of them much better than the French girls or the German girls. But the world they were in was not the world he was in. He would like to have one of them. But it was not worth it. They were such a nice pattern. He liked the pattern. It was exciting. But he would not go through all the talking. He did not want one badly enough. He liked to look at them all, though. It was not worth it.[6]

So much for Krebs: now open Miss Stein and "meet" Melanctha.

Rose was lazy but not dirty, and Sam was careful but not fussy, and then there was Melanctha. . . . When Rose's baby was coming to be born, Rose came to stay in the house where Melanctha Herbert lived just then, . . . Rose went there to stay, so that she might have the doctor from the hospital. . . . Melanctha Herbert had not made her life all simple like Rose Johnson. Melanctha had not found it easy with herself to make her wants and what she had, agree.

Melanctha Herbert was always losing what she had in wanting all the things she saw. Melanctha was always being left when she was not leaving others.

Melanctha Herbert always loved too hard and much too often. She was always full with mystery and subtle movements . . . etc., etc., etc.[7]

Or here is a typical bit from *Composition as Explanation*:

There is singularly nothing that makes a difference in beginning and in the middle and in ending except that each generation has something different at which they are all looking. By this I mean so simply that anybody knows it that composition is the difference which makes each and all of them then different from other generations and this is what makes everything different otherwise they are all alike and everybody knows it because everybody says it.[8]

There is no possibility, I am afraid, of slurring over this. It is just a thing that you have to accept as an unfortunate handicap in an artist who is in some respects above praise. Sometimes it is less pronounced, there are occasions when it is *almost* absent—Krebs, for instance, is a full-blooded example of Hemingway steining away for all he is worth. But it is never quite absent.

How much does it matter? If we blot out Gertrude Stein, and suppose she does not exist, does this part of Hemingway's equipment help or not? We must answer *Yes* I think. It does seem to help a good

[6] *In Our Time*, pp. 92, 94. Ernest Hemingway.
[7] *Three Lives*, p. 89. Gertrude Stein.
[8] *Composition as Explanation* (p. 5). Gertrude Stein.

deal: many of his best effects are obtained by means of it. It is so
much a part of his craft, indeed, that it is difficult now to imagine
Hemingway without this mannerism. He has never taken it over into
a gibbering and baboonish stage as has Miss Stein. He has kept it
as a valuable oddity, even if a flagrantly borrowed one—ever present
it is true, but one to which we can easily get used and come to like
even as a delightfully clumsy engine of innocence. I don't mind it
very much.

To say that, near to communism as we all are, it cannot matter,
and is indeed praiseworthy, for a celebrated artist to take over, lock,
stock and barrel from another artist the very thing for which he is
mainly known, seems to me to be going too far in the denial of the
person, or the individual—especially as in a case of this sort, the trick
is after all, in the first instance, a *personal* trick. Such a practice must
result, if universally indulged in, in hybrid forms or monstrosities.

And my main criticism, indeed, of the *steining* of Hemingway is
that it does impose upon him an ethos—*the Stein ethos,* as it might
be called. With Stein's bag of tricks he also takes over a *Weltan-
shauung,* which may not at all be his, and does in fact seem to
contradict his major personal quality. This infantile, dull-witted,
dreamy stutter compels whoever uses it to conform to the infantile,
dull-witted type. He passes over into the category of *those to whom
things are done,* from that of those who execute—if the latter is indeed
where he originally belonged. One might even go so far as to say
that this brilliant Jewish lady had made a *clown* of him by teaching
Ernest Hemingway her baby-talk! So it is a pity. And it is very difficult
to know where Hemingway proper begins and Stein leaves off as an
artist. It is an uncomfortable situation for the critic, especially for
one who "has a weakness" for the male member of this strange spiritual partnership, and very much prefers him to the female.

Hemingway's two principal books, *The Sun Also Rises* (for English
publication called *Fiesta*) and *Farewell to Arms,* are delivered in the
first person singular. What that involves may not be at once apparent
to those who have not given much attention to literary composition.
But it is not at all difficult to explain. Suppose you, Raymond Robinson, sit down to write a romance; subject-matter, the War. You get
your "I" started off, say just before the outbreak of war, and then
there is the outbreak, and then "I flew to the nearest recruiting station
and joined the army" you write. Then the "I" goes off to the Western
Front (or the Italian Front) and you will find yourself writing "I
seized the Boche by the throat with one hand and shot him in the
stomach with the other," or whatever it is you imagine your "I" as
doing. But this "I," the reader will learn, does not bear the name

on the title page, namely Raymond Robinson. He is called Geoffrey Jones. The reader will think, "that is only a thin disguise. It is Robinson's personal experience all right!"

Now this difficulty (if it be a difficulty) is very much enhanced if (for some reason) Geoffrey Jones is *always* doing exactly the things that Raymond Robinson is known to have done. If Raymond Robinson fought gallantly at Caporetto, for instance, then Geoffrey Jones—with the choice of a whole earth at war to choose from—is at Caporetto too. If Raymond Robinson takes to the sport of bull-fighting, sure enough Geoffrey Jones—the "I" of the novel—is there in the bull-ring too, as the night follows day. This, in fine, has been the case with Hemingway and *his* First-person-singular.

Evidently, in this situation—possessing a First-person-singular that invariably copies you in this flattering way—something must be done about it. The *First-person-singular* has to be endowed so palpably with qualities that could by no stretch of the imagination belong to its author that no confusion is possible. Upon this principle the "I" of *The Sun Also Rises* is described as sexually impotent, which is a complete alibi, of course, for Hemingway.

But there is more than this. The sort of First-person-singular that Hemingway invariably invokes is a dull-witted, bovine, monosyllabic simpleton. This lethargic and stuttering dummy he conducts, or pushes from behind, through all the scenes that interest him. This burlesque First-person-singular behaves in them like a moronesque version of his brilliant author. He *Steins* up and down the world, with the big lustreless ruminatory orbs of a Picasso doll-woman (of the semi-classic type Picasso patented, with enormous hands and feet). It is, in short, the very dummy that is required for the literary mannerism of Miss Stein! It is the incarnation of the Stein-stutter—the male incarnation, it is understood.

But this constipated, baffled "frustrated"—yes, deeply and Freudianly 'frustrated'—this wooden-headed, leaden-witted, heavy-footed, loutish and oafish marionette—peering dully out into the surrounding universe like a great big bloated five-year-old—pointing at this and pointing at that—uttering simply "CAT!"—"HAT!"—"FOOD!"—"SWEETIE!"—is, as a companion, infectious. His author has perhaps not been quite immune. Seen for ever through his nursery spectacles, the values of life accommodate themselves, even in the mind of his author, to the limitations and peculiar requirements of this highly idiosyncratic puppet.

So the political aspects of Hemingway's work (if, as I started by saying, one can employ such a word as *political* in connection with a thing is so divorced from reality as a super-innocent, queerly-sensitive, village-idiot of a few words and fewer ideas) have to be sought, if anywhere, in the personality of this *First-person-singular,* imposed upon him largely by the Stein-manner.

We can return to the folk-prose problem now and face all the questions that the "done gones" and "sorta gonnas" present. Mr. H. L. Mencken in his well-known, extremely competent and exhaustive treatise, *The American Language* (a classic in this field of research, first published fifteen years ago) affirmed that the American dialect had not yet come to the stage where it could be said to have acquired charm for "the purists." If used (at that time) in narrative literature it still possessed only the status of a disagreeable and socially-inferior jargon, like the cockney occurring in a Dickens novel—or as it is still mostly used in William Faulkner's novels, never outside of inverted commas; the novelist, having invoked it to convey the manner of speech of his rustic or provincial puppets, steps smartly away and resumes the narrative in the language of Macaulay or Horace Walpole, more or less.

"In so far as it is apprehended at all," Mencken wrote in 1920, "it is only in the sense that Irish-English was apprehended a generation ago—that is, as something uncouth and comic. But that is the way that new dialects always come in—through a drum-fire of cackles. Given the poet, there may suddenly come a day when our *theirns* and *would 'a hads* will take on the barbaric stateliness of the peasant locution of old Maurya in 'Riders to the Sea.' " [9]

The reason that the dialect of the Arran Islands, or that used by Robert Burns, was so different from cockney or from the English educated speech was because it was a mixture of English and another language, Gaelic or lowland Scotch, and with the intermixture of foreign words went a literal translation of foreign idioms and the distortions arrived at by a tongue accustomed to another language. It was "broken-English," in other words, not "low-English," or slum-English, as is cockney.

Americans are today un-English in blood—whatever names they may bear: and in view of this it is surprising how intact the English language remains in the United States. But the *Beach-la-mar*, as he calls it, to which Mencken is referring above, is as it were the cockney of America. It has this great advantage over cockney, that it is fed with a great variety of immigrant words. It is, however, fundamentally *a class-jargon;* not a jargon resulting from difference of race, and consequently of speech. It is the *patois* of the "poor white," the negro, or the uneducated immigrant. It is not the language spoken by Mrs. Alice Roosevelt Longworth, for instance, or by Ernest Hemingway for

[9] *The American Language,* p. 396.

that matter. But it is very *American*. And it is a *patois*, a fairly good rendering of which any American is competent to give. And you have read above the affectionate way Mencken refers to *our* "theirns" and "would 'a hads."

English as spoken in America is more vigorous and expressive than Oxford English, I think. It is easy to mistake a native from the wilds of Dorsetshire for an American, I have found: and were "educated" English used upon a good strong reverberant Dorsetshire basis, for instance, it would be all to the good, it is my opinion. Raleigh, Drake, and the rest of them, must have talked rather like that.

But with cockney it is not at all the same thing. There you get a degradation of English—it is *proletariat*, city-slum English, like Dublin-slum English. That is in a different category altogether to the weighty, rapid, and expressive torrent of the best Dorsetshire talk; and, as I have said, the *best* American is in the same category as the Dorsetshire—or as non-slum Irish—a good, sound accent, too. But the question to be answered is whether the *Beach-la-mar* Mr. Mencken has in mind is not too much the deteriorated pidgin tongue of the United States; and whether, if that is *affectioné* too much by the *literati*—as being the most *American* thing available, like a jazz— it is not going to be a vulgar corruption, which will vulgarize, as well as enrich, the tongue. So far it exists generally in inverted commas, as in Mr. Faulkner's books. Is it to be let out or not? A question for Americans.

For fifty years dialect-American has tended, what with negro and immigrant pressure, to simplify itself grammatically, and I suppose is still doing so at this moment.

His (the immigrant's) linguistic habits and limitations have to be reckoned with in dealing with him and the concessions thus made necessary have a very ponderable influence upon the general speech. Of much importance is the support given to the native tendency by the foreigner's incapacity for employing (or even comprehending) syntax of any complexity, or words not of the simplest. This is the tendency towards succinctness and clarity, at whatever sacrifice of grace. One English observer, Sidney Low, puts the chief blame for the general explosiveness of American upon the immigrant, who must be communicated with in the plainest words available, and is not socially worthy of the suavity of circumlocution anyhow. In his turn the immigrant seizes upon these plainest words as upon a sort of convenient Lingua Franca—his quick adoption of *damn* as a universal adjective is traditional—and throws his influence upon the side of the underlying speech habit when he gets on in the vulgate. Many characteristic Americanisms of the sort to stagger lexicographers—for example, *near-silk*—have come from Jews, whose progress in business is a good deal faster than their progress in English.

While England was a uniquely powerful empire-state, ruled by an aristocratic caste, its influence upon the speech as upon the psychology of the American ex-colonies was overwhelming. But today that ascendancy has almost entirely vanished. The aristocratic caste is nothing but a shadow of itself, the cinema has brought the American scene and the American dialect nightly into the heart of England, and the "Americanizing" process is far advanced. "Done gones," "good guys" and "buddies" sprout upon the lips of cockney children as readily as upon those to the manner born, of New York or Chicago: and there is no politically-powerful literate class any longer now, in our British "Banker's Olympus," to confer prestige upon an exact and intelligent selective speech. Americanization—which is also for England, at least, proletarianization—is too far advanced to require underlining, even for people who fail usually to recognize anything until it has been in existence for a quarter of a century.

But if America has come to England, there has been no reciprocal movement of England into the United States: indeed, with the new American nationalism, England is deliberately kept out: and all the great influence that England exerted formerly—merely by being there and speaking the same tongue and sharing the same fundamental political principles—that is today a thing of the past. So the situation is this, as far as our common language is concerned: the destiny of England and the United States of America is more than ever one. But it is now the American influence that is paramount. The tables have effectively been turned in that respect.

But there is a larger issue even than that local to the English-speaking nations. English is of all languages the simplest grammatically and the easiest to make into a *Beach-la-mar* or *pidgin* tongue. Whether this fact, combined with its "extraordinary tendency to degenerate into slang of every kind," is against it, is of some importance for the future—for it will have less and less grammar, obviously, and more and more cosmopolitan slang.—Mr. Mencken is of opinion that a language cannot be too simple—he is all for *Beach-la-mar*. The path towards analysis and the elimination of inflection, has been trod by English so thoroughly that, in its American form, it should today win the race for a universal volapuk. Indeed, as Mr. Mencken says, "the foreigner essaying it, indeed, finds his chief difficulty, not in mastering its forms, but in grasping its lack of form. He doesn't have to learn a new and complex grammar; what he has to do is to forget grammar. Once he has done so, the rest is a mere matter of acquiring a vocabulary."

There is, it is true, the difficulty of the vowel sounds: but that is easily settled. Standard English possesses nineteen distinct vowel sounds: no other living European tongue except Portuguese, so Mr. Mencken says, possesses so many. Modern Greek, for instance, can only boast of five, we are told. "The (American) immigrant, facing all these vowels, finds some of them quite impossible: the Russian Jew, for example, cannot manage *ur*. As a result, he tends to employ a neutralized vowel in the situations which present difficulties, and this neutralized vowel, supported by the slip-shod speech-habits of the native proletariat, makes steady progress."

That that "neutralized vowel" has made great progress in America no one would deny who has been there; and, starting in the natural language-difficulties of the Central European immigrant, the above-mentioned "neutralized vowel" will make its way over here in due course, who can doubt it? These vowels must be watched. *Watch your vowels* should be our next national slogan! The fatal grammatical easiness of English is responsible, however, for such problems as these, as much as the growing impressionability of the English nation, and the proletarianization, rather than the reverse, of the American.

As long ago as 1910 an English traveller, Mr. Alexander Thompson, in a book called *Japan for a Week,* expresses himself as follows:

> It was only on reaching Italy that I began fully to realize this wonderful thing, that for nearly six weeks, on a German ship, in a journey of nearly ten thousand miles, we had heard little of any language but English! It is an amazing thing when one thinks of it.
>
> In Japan most of the tradespeople spoke English. At Shanghai, at Hong-Kong, at Singapore, at Penang, at Colombo, at Suez, at Port Said —all the way home to the Italian ports, the language of all the ship's traffic, the language of such discourse as the passengers held with natives, most of the language on board ship itself, was English.
>
> The German captain of our ship spoke English more often than German. All his officers spoke English.
>
> The Chinese man-o'-war's men who conveyed the Chinese prince on board at Shanghai, received commands and exchanged commands with our German sailors in English. The Chinese mandarins in their conversations with the ships' officers invariably spoke English. They use the same ideographs in writing as the Japanese, but to talk to our Japanese passengers they had to speak English. Nay, coming as they did from various provinces of the Empire, where the language greatly differs, they found it most convenient in conversation among themselves to speak English.

If you place side by side the unfortunate impressionability of Hemingway, which caused him to adopt integrally the half-wit simplicity of repetitive biblical diction patented by Miss Stein, and that other fact that Mr. Hemingway, being an American nationalist by temperament, is inclined to gravitate stylistically towards the national underdog dialect, in the last resort to the kind of *Beach-la-mar* I have been discussing, you have the two principal factors in Hemingway as artist in prose-fiction, to make of what you can.

Take up any book of his, again, and open it at random: you will find a page of stuff that is, considered in isolation, valueless as writing. It is not written: it is lifted out of Nature and very artfully and adroitly tumbled out upon the page: it is the brute material of every-day proletarian speech and feeling. The *matière* is cheap and coarse: but not because it is proletarian speech merely, but because it is *the prose of reality*—the prose of the street-car or the provincial news-paper or the five and ten cent store. I have just opened *Farewell to Arms* entirely at random, for instance, and this is what I find:

"If you had any foreign bodies in your legs they would set up an inflammation and you'd have fever."

"All right," I said. "We'll see what comes out."

She went out of the room and came back with the old nurse of the early morning. Together they made the bed with me in it. That was new to me and an admirable proceeding.

"Who is in charge here?"

"Miss Van Campen."

"How many nurses are there?"

"Just us two."

"Won't there be more?"

"Some more are coming."

"When will they get here?"

"I don't know. You ask a great many questions for a sick boy."

"I'm not sick." I said, "I'm wounded."

They had finished making the bed and I lay with a clean, smooth sheet under me and another sheet over me. Mrs. Walker went out and came back with a pyjama jacket. They put that on me and I felt very clean and dressed.

"You're awfully nice to me," I said. The nurse called Miss Gage gig-gled. "Could I have a drink of water?" I asked.

"Certainly. Then you can have breakfast."

"I don't want breakfast. Can I have the shutters opened, please?"

The light had been dim in the room and when the shutters were opened it was bright sunlight, and I looked out on a balcony and be-yond were the tiled roofs of houses and chimneys and the sky very blue.

"Don't you know when the other nurses are coming?"

"Why? Don't we take good care of you?"

"You're very nice."

"Would you like to use the bedpan?"

"I might try."

They helped me and held me up, but it was not any use. Afterward I lay and looked out the open doors on to the balcony.

"When does the doctor come?"

It is not writing, if you like. When I read *Farewell to Arms* doubtless I read this page as I came to it, just as I should watch scenes unfolding on the screen in the cinema, without pictorial criticism; and it, page eighly-three, contributed its fraction to the general effect: and when I had finished the book I thought it a very good book. By that I meant that the cumulative effect was impressive, as *the events themselves* would be. Or it is like reading a newspaper, day by day, about some matter of absorbing interest—say the reports of a divorce, murder, or libel action. If you say *anyone could write it,* you are mistaken there, because, to obtain that smooth effect, of commonplace reality, there must be no sentimental or other heightening, the number of words expended must be proportionate to the importance and the length of the respective phases of the action, and any false move or overstatement would at once stand out and tell against it. If an inferior reporter to Hemingway took up the pen, that fact would at once be detected by a person sensitive to reality.

It is an art, then, from this standpoint, like the cinema, or like those "modernist" still-life pictures in which, in place of *painting* a match box upon the canvas, a piece of actual match box is stuck on. A recent example of this (I choose it because a good many people will have seen it) is the cover design of the French periodical *Minotaure,* in which Picasso has pasted and tacked various things together, sticking a line drawing of the Minotaur in the middle. Hemingway's is a poster-art, in this sense: or a *cinema in words. The steining* in the text of Hemingway is as it were the hand-made part—if we are considering it as "super-realist" design: a manipulation of the photograph if we are regarding it as a film.

If you say that this is not the way that Dante wrote, that these are not artistically permanent creations—or not permanent in the sense of a verse of Bishop King, or a page of Gulliver, I agree. But it is what we have got: there is actually *bad* and *good* of this kind; and I for my part enjoy what I regard as the good, without worrying any more about it than that.

That a particular phase in the life of humanity is implicit in this art is certain. It is one of the first fruits of the *proletarianization* which, as a result of the amazing revolutions in the technique of industry, we are all undergoing, whether we like it or not. But this purely political, or sociological side to the question can be brought out, I believe, with great vividness by a quotation. Here, for instance, is a fragment of a story of a mutiny at sea:

I opened the door a little, about two inches, and saw there was a rope round the companion, which prevented the doors opening. Big Harry and Lips asked me what I wanted. I said I wanted to go down to the galley. Big Harry said: "Plenty of time between this and eight o'clock; you stop down below." I then went into the chief mate's room, which was the nearest to me. There was nobody there. I went to the second mate's room, he was not there. I went to the captain's pillow, it was standing up in his bed, and I found two revolvers loaded, one with six shots and one with four. I took possession of them and put them in my pockets. I then stood on the cabin table in the after cabin, and lifted the skylight up and tried to get out there. Renken was standing at the wheel, and he called out, "Come aft, boys, the steward is coming out of the skylight." I then closed the skylight and came down again. The after-skylight was close to the wheel, about 10 feet as near as I could guess. I could see him. The light used for the compass is in the skylight, and the wheel is in the back of it. The light is fastened to the skylight to light the compass, and the compass is just in front of the wheel. Before I could get the skylight closed I heard their steps coming aft, and I went down into the cabin and told the boy to light a fire. Shortly afterwards I heard five shots fired on deck . . . about a second afterwards the same as if somebody was running on deck. I could not judge which way they were running; the noise on the deck, and the vessel being in ballast, you could hear as well aft as forward. That was about twenty minutes after hearing the captain call out. I put the revolvers away in my locker. I then took it into my head to take the revolvers into my possession and chance it; if the men came down to me to do anything wrong, to save myself. I put them in my pockets, one on each side. About 5.30 Green, the boatswain, came down first, and French Peter, Big Harry, and all the other lot followed. The deck was left without anybody, and the wheel too, they came into the cabin; Trousillot was there as well. They did not speak at first. The first thing they did was to rub me over. They could not feel anything. I had the two revolvers with me, but they did not feel them. French Peter and Big Harry felt me over. All the others were present. Green said, "Well, steward, we have finished now." I said, "What the hell did you finish?" He said, "We have finished captain, mate and second." He said, "We got our mind made up to go to Greece; if you like to save your own life you had better take charge of the ship and bring us to Greece. You bring us to Gibraltar, we will find Greece: you bring us there you will be all right, steward. We will take the boats when we get to Greece, and take the sails and everything into the boats, and sell them ashore and divide the money between ourselves. You will have your share, the same as anybody else; the charts and sextants, and all that belongs to the navigation, you can have. Me and my cousin, Johny Moore, have got a rich uncle; he will buy everything. We will scuttle the ship. My uncle is a large owner there of some ships. We will see you right, that you will be master of one of those vessels." I said, "Well, men, come on deck and get them braces ready, and I hope you will agree and also obey my orders!" The other men said, "All right, steward, very good, very good, steward, you do right." That was all I could hear from them, from everybody. The conversation between me and Green was in English, and everybody standing round. He spoke to the other men in Greek. What he said I don't know. I said, "Where are the bodies? Where is the captain?" Green said, "Oh they are all right, they are overboard," and all the men said the same. . . ." [10]

That is not by Hemingway, though it quite well might be. I should not be able to tell it was not by Hemingway if it were shown me as a fragment. But this is by him:

Across the bay they found the other boat beached. Uncle George was smoking a cigar in the dark. The young Indian pulled the boat way up the beach. Uncle George gave both the Indians cigars. They walked up from the beach through a meadow that was soaking wet with dew, following the young Indian who carried a lantern. Then they went into the woods and followed a trail that led to the logging road that ran back into the hills. It was much lighter on the logging road as the timber was cut away on both sides. The young Indian stopped and blew out his lantern and they all walked on along the road.

They came around a bend and a dog came out barking. Ahead were the lights of the shanties where the Indian bark-peelers lived. More dogs rushed out at them. The two Indians sent them back to the shanties. In the shanty nearest the road there was a light in the window. An old woman stood in the doorway holding a lamp.

Inside on a wooden bunk lay a young Indian woman. She had been trying to have her baby for two days. All the old women in the camp had been helping her. The men had moved off up the road to sit in the dark and smoke out of range of the noise she made. She screamed just as Nick and the two Indians followed his father and Uncle George into the shanty. She lay in the lower bunk, very big under a quilt. Her head was turned to one side. In the upper bunk was her husband. He had cut his foot very badly with an axe three days before. He was smoking a pipe. The room smelled very bad. Nick's father ordered some water to be put on the stove, while it was heating he spoke to Nick. "This lady is going to have a baby, Nick," he said. "I know," said Nick. "You don' know," said his father. "Listen to me. What she is going through is called being in labour. The baby wants to be born and she wants it to be born. All her muscles are trying to get the baby born. That is what is happening when she screams." "I see," Nick said. Just then the woman cried out.[11]

The first of these two passages is from a book entitled *Forty Years in the Old Bailey*. It is the account of a mutiny and murder on the high seas, the trial occurring on May 3 and 4, 1876. It was evidence verbatim of one Constant von Hoydonck, a Belgian, twenty-five years of age, who joined the vessel *Lennie* at Antwerp, as chief steward, on October 22. This is a *Querschnitt*, a slice, of 'real life': and how close Hemingway

[10] *Forty Years at the Old Bailey*. F. Lamb.
[11] *In Our Time*. Ernest Hemingway.

is to such material as this can be seen by comparing it with the second passage out of *In Our Time*.

That, I think, should put you in possession of all that is essential for an understanding of the work of this very notable artist: an understanding I mean; I do not mean that, as a work of art, a book of his should be approached in this critical and anatomizing spirit. That is another matter. Where the "politics" come in I suppose by this time you will have gathered. This is the voice of the "folk," of the masses, who are the cannon-fodder, the cattle outside the slaughter-house, serenely chewing the cud—*of those to whom things are done,* in contrast to those who have executive will and intelligence. It is itself innocent of politics—one might almost add alas! That does not affect its quality as art. The expression of the soul of the dumb ox would have a penetrating beauty of its own, if it were uttered with genius—with bovine genius (and in the case of Hemingway that is what has happened): just as much as would the folk-song of the baboon, or of the "Praying Mantis." But where the politics crop up is that if we take this to be the typical art of a civilization—and there is no serious writer who stands higher in Anglo-Saxony today than does Ernest Hemingway—then we are by the same token saying something very definite about that civilization.

Ciphers at the Front

by D. S. Savage

I

Ernest Hemingway is known as the author of a number of miscellaneous novels and short stories, as well as two books on blood sports. His best-known works, however, are two "novels of love and war," *A Farewell to Arms* and *For Whom the Bell Tolls,* and his significant development, such as it is (for only in a very special sense can he be said to develop at all), may best be seen by a comparison of those two works. In the second section of this essay such a comparison will be made, but to begin with I propose to examine the essential or typical qualities of the Hemingway presented to us in the general body of his work.

Hemingway first received attention, when he was publishing his earlier stories, as a *stylist*. And this is interesting, for the content of his stories is in great part crude violent action, not essentially dissimilar from the subject-matter of the stories found in the cheap "pulp" magazines of a primarily masculine appeal. It may reasonably be assumed that Hemingway satisfies, on a somewhat higher level of culture or of sophistication, the same imaginative cravings fed among the semiliterate proletarian masses of England and America by such productions as *War Aces* and *Action Stories*. The difference is that where the writer of "pulp" stories is writing deliberately to a known consumer-demand, and where his products are, consequently, mechanical and lacking in psychological content, Hemingway is consciously an artist, writing to achieve an aesthetic effect, and is himself, therefore, emotionally involved in his own work. It follows that in his stories the emphasis is not, as in the "pulp" magazines, entirely on the crude, mechanical action, taking place in a complete psychic vacuum. The psychological implications of the violence of the "pulp" mentality are made explicit. In reading Hemingway we are made aware that the

"Ciphers at the Front" (*Editor's title*). *From* The Withered Branch *by D. S. Savage* (London: Eyre & Spottiswoode, Ltd., *1950*), *pp. 23–36. Copyright © 1950 by D. S. Savage. Reprinted by permission of the author.*

violent action itself, of so many of his stories, arises from the need for the alleviation of a prior and underlying psychic vacuity—an emotional state which is sometimes in his work suggested with great skill.

Hemingway is, within very narrow limits, a stylist who has brought to something like perfection a curt, unemotional, factual style which is an attempt at the objective presentation of experience. A bare, dispassionate reporting of external actions is all that Hemingway as a rule attempts in presenting his characters and incidents. His typical central character, his "I," may be described generally as a bare consciousness stripped to the human minimum, impassively recording the objective data of experience. He has no contact with ideas, no visible emotions, no hopes for the future, and no memory. He is, as far as it is possible to be so, a *de-personalized* being.

A brief glance at Hemingway's first book, a collection of tales entitled *In Our Time* (1925), will give us some notion of the essentials of his attitude and his equipment as a writer. These tales are really a series of brief, laconic sketches from the life of a man, together forming a fragmentary novel. The settings of the sketches alternate between the American countryside of Nick's boyhood, the scenes of war on the Italian Front, and post-war America and Europe. The action, however, is slight and subordinated to the predominant mood, conveyed with admirable honesty and artistic scrupulousness, which is one of utter and complete negation, almost of nihilism. "Nick," wrote D. H. Lawrence, reviewing the book on its appearance in England, "is a type one meets in the more wild and woolly regions of the United States. He is the remains of the lone trapper and cowboy. Nowadays, he is educated, and through with everything. It is a state of conscious, accepted indifference to everything except freedom from work and the moment's interest. Nothing matters. Everything happens. Avoid one thing only: getting connected up. If you get held by anything, break it. Don't get away with the idea of getting somewhere else. Just get away, for the sake of getting away. Beat it! . . . His young love-affair ends as one throws a cigarette-end away. 'It isn't fun any more.' 'Everything's gone to hell inside me . . . .' He doesn't love anybody, and it nauseates him to have to pretend he does. He doesn't even *want* to love anybody; he doesn't want to go anywhere; he doesn't want to do anything. He wants just to lounge around and maintain a healthy state of nothingness inside himself, and an attitude of negation to everything outside himself. And why shouldn't he, since that is exactly and sincerely what he feels?"

In Our Time, like much other of Hemingway's work, is fairly transparently autobiographical; it reads for the most part like a literal, though of course uncommonly discriminating, transcription of bare experience. A simple stylist like Hemingway, in search of a material upon which to exercise and develop his skill, would naturally turn first of all to the material nearest to hand—i.e. the material of simple personal experience. But a mind of Hemingway's negative and static quality will, it is evident, be unable to furnish sufficient material of a straight-forward autobiographical kind for the simple craftsman to work on. Unlike a novelist of more complex and active mentality, gifted with psychological insight and the power to project, through the creation of character, a personal vision of experience—for whom, consequently, there would be no abrupt transition from "autobiography" to "fiction"—Hemingway is forced to turn for material to the plane, as I have said, of the "pulp" magazine. His peculiarly negative view of human life quite naturally leads him to project his vision, when he leaves straight autobiography, into figures drawn from the lowest stratum of human existence, where life is lived as near as possible on an animal, mechanical level.

Here is a passage, from a work which is evidently of an autobiographical character rather than not, which has the advantage of representing Hemingway's characteristic factual style while at the same time presenting a fragment of typical subject-matter, which has its own implications on the human, moral plane. It is an incident in a military retreat from the novel *A Farewell to Arms*.

> "I order you to cut brush," I said. They turned and started down the road.
> "Halt," I said. They kept on down the muddy road, the hedge on either side. "I order you to halt," I called. They went a little faster. I opened up my holster, took the pistol, aimed at the one who had talked the most, and fired. I missed and they both started to run; I shot three times and dropped one. The other went through the hedge and was out of sight. I fired at him through the hedge as he ran across the field. The pistol clicked empty and I put in another clip. I saw it was too far to shoot at the second sergeant. He was far across the field, running, his head held low. I commenced to reload the empty clip. Bonello came up.
> "Let me go finish him," he said. I handed him the pistol and he walked down to where the sergeant of engineers lay face down across the road. Bonello leaned over, put the pistol against the man's head and pulled the trigger. The pistol did not fire.
> "You have to cock it," I said. He cocked and fired twice. He took hold of the sergeant's legs and pulled him to the side of the road so he lay beside the hedge. He came back and handed me the pistol.
> "The son of a bitch," he said.

The transition from writing on this level to the subsequent and alternative level of the human underworld involves no very considerable descent, it is clear. The following is from a sketch entitled "The Killers."

"What are you going to kill Ole Andreson for? What did he ever do to you?"

"He never had a chance to do anything to us. He never even seen us."

"And he's only going to see us once," Al said from the kitchen.

"What are you going to kill him for, then?" George asked.

"We're killing him for a friend. Just to oblige a friend, bright boy."

"Shut up," said Al from the kitchen. "You talk too goddam much."

"Well, I got to keep bright boy amused. Don't I, bright boy."

"You talk too damn much," Al said. "The nigger and my bright boy are amusing themselves. I got them tied up like a couple of girl friends in the convent." [1]

The wider implications of the above examples of Hemingway's manner and matter are, of course, related to the almost complete extrusion of his vision of life upon the plane of the external—the plane of extreme objectivization where experience is alienated from its subject. To deprive life of its inwardness, and to see men, not as personalities, but as objects, as things, is to open the door, not for a morally condemnable cruelty or brutality so much as for an even more devastating, because cold and spiritless, contempt of human values and of human life, which puts killing a man on the same level of actuality as cooking an egg or blacking one's boots. For good measure, I give a further, and incidentally later, example of Hemingway's objective eye for violence.

The other fellow pulled the one who was hit back by the legs to behind the wagon, and I saw the nigger getting his face down on the paving to give them another burst. Then I saw old Pancho come around the corner of the wagon and step into the lee of the horse that was still up. He stepped clear of the horse, his face white as a dirty sheet, and got the chauffeur with the big Luger he had; holding it in both hands to keep it steady. He shot twice over the nigger's head, coming on, and once low.

He hit a tyre on the car because I saw dust blowing in a spurt on the street as the air came out, and at ten feet the nigger shot him in the belly with the Tommy gun, with what must have been the last shot in it because I saw him throw it down, and old Pancho sat down hard and went over forwards. He was trying to come up, still holding on to the Luger, only he couldn't get his head up, when the nigger took the shot gun that was lying against the wheel of the car by the chauffeur and blew the side of his head off. Some nigger. [2]

Hemingway's de-personalized style, it appears, is the result of no detached, arbitrary choice. It is a style actually perfectly expressive of his outlook on life. In the flat, chaotic, elementary world into which we are introduced by Hemingway's fiction, everything is objectivized: in-

---

[1] *Men Without Women* (1928).
[2] *To Have and Have Not* (1937).

wardness, subjectivity, is eliminated, and man himself is made into an object, a thing. This entire extrusion of personality into the outward sensational world makes his characters the inwardly-passive victims of a meaningless determinism. They inhabit a world which, because it has been voided of inwardness, is entirely without significance. The Hemingway character is a creature without religion, morality, politics, culture or history—without any of those aspects, that is to say, of the distinctively human existence.

Such an outlook is a peculiar one in a writer because it precludes the possibility of organic and interesting development. The Hemingway world is one of mechanical repetition, and in the series of Hemingway's nine or ten books there is no inward continuity to keep pace with the chronological sequence. It is therefore impossible to consider Hemingway as if there were some coherently developing pattern running through his progress as a writer. That there is a development of some kind, a *static* development, so to speak, I shall presently try to show. But the critic, I think, need feel no special obligation to consider Hemingway's works as a sequence. The pattern is essentially a fixed one, made by the running of the mind in a deterministic groove. Apart from the two "war and love" novels which must be examined separately, there is only one book which throws any special light on Hemingway's mind, and that is the book on the Spanish bullfight entitled *Death in the Afternoon,* which serves the purpose of showing in a simple and explicit form Hemingway's fascinated preoccupation, which up to now I have refrained from commenting on, with the fact of death.

The profound spiritual inertia, the inner vacancy and impotence, which is a mark of all Hemingway's projected characters, issues in a deadening sense of boredom and negation which can only be relieved by violent, though still essentially meaningless, activity. The more violent the activity, the greater the relief from the sickening vertigo of boredom. But activity of this kind is in fact a drug, and like most other kinds of drug, for its effect to be maintained it must be taken in constantly increasing quantities. Ultimately, however, the state of boredom, certainly one of the most horrible of human experiences, reduces itself not merely to the absence of meaning, but to the total absence of a sense of life. Indeed, it is a feature of violent action that while it cannot produce a convincing sense of meaningfulness, it can at any rate produce an illusory sense of *life*. Violent action itself, however, is almost always destructive action. Its end is in death. And, ultimately, when the sense of life itself vanishes, there is only one way in which it may be recaptured, and that is by the violent, absolute contrast of life with death. Life regains its "reality" in such cases—becomes, that is, aesthetically sensational and vivid in itself—only when it is brought up against the stark, black negation of the void.

Writing, in *Death in the Afternoon*, of his early interest in the bullfight, Hemingway says:

> I was trying to write then and I found the greatest difficulty, aside from knowing truly what you really felt, rather than what you were supposed to feel, and had been taught to feel, was to put down what really happened in action; what the actual things were which produced the emotion you experienced.
>
> . . . The only place where you could see life and death, i.e. violent death now that the wars were over, was in the bull ring and I wanted very much to go to Spain where I could study it. I was trying to learn to write, commencing with the simplest things, and one of the simplest things of all and the most fundamental is violent death. . . .
>
> So far, about morals, I know only that what is moral is what you feel good after and what is immoral is what you feel bad after and judged by these moral standards, which I do not defend, the bullfight is very moral to me because I feel very fine while it is going on and have a feeling of life and death and mortality and immortality, and after it is over I feel very sad but very fine.

Death in the Afternoon, which partakes of the nature of an esoteric introduction to a blood-cult, is written throughout in a tone of alternating naïve solemnity and cynical jocularity. But here, he seems to imply, in a senseless, mechanical and phoney world, is something which seems to be real and meaningful, and which may somehow be approached in a way which will impart a sense of significance and reality to living.

> . . . Someone with English blood has written: "Life is real; life is earnest; and the grave is not its goal." And where did they bury him? and what became of the reality and the earnestness? The people of Castilla have great common sense. They could not produce a poet who would write a line like that. They know death is the unescapable reality, the one thing any man may be sure of; the only security; that it transcends all modern comforts and that with it you do not need a bath-tub in every American home, nor, when you have it, do you need the radio. They think a great deal about death, and when they have a religion they have one which believes that life is much shorter than death. Having this feeling they take an intelligent interest in death. . . .

Such passages as this do at least reveal the nature, whatever one may think of its value, of the chief preservative of Hemingway's significance as a writer, that kind of desperate honesty which, once the bottom has been knocked out of things by painful and horrifying experience, cannot rest content with the pusillanimous compromises with which most people afterwards patch up their lives, and which one detects in the revulsion from the "bath-tub in every American home," and in the manifest dread of any kind of "faking" (in writing as in bullfighting) which is displayed throughout the book. A glance at one further facet of Hemingway's personal outlook, and we can pass on from this brief survey of his typical work. In *Green Hills of Africa* (1936), a tedious description of a hunting trip, there are two passages which are of interest for the light they throw on Hemingway as a writer. The first concerns *subject*.

> I thought about Tolstoy and about what a great advantage an experience of war was to a writer. It was one of the major subjects and certainly one of the hardest to write truly of, and those writers who had not seen it were always very jealous and tried to make it seem unimportant, or abnormal, or a disease as a subject, while, really, it was just something quite irreplaceable that they had missed.

The second concerns, not subject, and not technique, exactly, but the writer's intention:

> The reason every one now tries to avoid it, to deny that it is important, to make it seem vain to try to do it, is because it is so difficult. Too many factors must combine to make it possible. . . . The kind of writing that can be done. How far prose can be carried if anyone is serious enough and has luck. There is a fourth and fifth dimension that can be gotten. [And if a writer can get this] . . . Then nothing else matters. It is more important than anything he can do. The chances are, of course, that he will fail. But there is a chance that he succeeds. . . . It is much more difficult than poetry. It is a prose that has never been written. But it can be written, without tricks and without cheating. With nothing that will go bad afterwards. . . . First, there must be talent, much talent. Talent such as Kipling had. Then there must be discipline. The discipline of Flaubert. Then there must be the conception of what it can be and an absolute conscience as unchanging as the standard meter in Paris, to prevent faking. Then the writer must be intelligent and disinterested and above all he must survive.

Such, or something such, is the conception of himself which Hemingway would like to project into the public mind. It is an interesting conception.

A novelist, of admitted literary merit, who lacks all the equipment generally expected of a practitioner of his art except a certain artistic scrupulousness and poetic sense, is something of a phenomenon. And while one would hardly suppose Hemingway could be considered as, intrinsically, a very important writer, yet, it is obvious, his purely symptomatic significance is considerable. For what does Hemingway represent but that, in a special form, which might be termed the *proletarianization* of literature: the adaptation of the technical artistic conscience to the sub-average human consciousness? Sociologically considered, Hemingway seems to me to epitomize a phase of culture in which all the inward values which have sustained that culture in the past are vanishing, and nothing much is left but the empty shell of civilization—the shell of technique. The characters of Hemingway reflect accurately the consciousness of the depersonalized modern man of the totalitarian era, from whom all inward sources have been withdrawn, who has become alienated from his experience and objectivized into his environment.

C. S. Lewis, in his *Preface to Paradise Lost,* drawing a distinction between the Primary Epic of Homer and the Secondary Epic of Virgil and Milton, points out that the former kind is deprived of the great subject possessed by the latter because "the mere endless up and down, the constant aimless alternations of glory and misery, which make up the terrible phenomenon called a Heroic Age," admit of no historical pattern or design, which can only be given "when some event can be held to effect a profound and more or less permanent change in the history of the world, as the founding of Rome did, or still more, the fall of man."

No one event is really very much more important than another. No achievement can be permanent: today we kill and feast, tomorrow we are killed, and our women led away as slaves. Nothing "stays put," nothing has a significance beyond the moment. Heroism and tragedy there are in plenty, therefore good stories in plenty; but no "large design that brings the world out of the good to ill." The total effect is not a pattern, but a kaleidoscope. . . . Primary Epic is great, but not with the greatness of the later kind. In Homer, its greatness lies in the human and personal tragedy built up against this background of meaningless flux. It is all the more tragic because there hangs over the heroic world a certain futility. "And here I sit in Troy," says Achilles to Priam, "afflicting you and your children." Not "protecting Greece," not even "winning glory," not called by any vocation to afflict Priam, but just doing it because that is the way things come about. . . . Only the style—the unwearying, unmoved, angelic speech of Homer—makes it endurable. Without that the *Iliad* would be a poem beside which the grimmest modern realism is child's play.

It does not seem far-fetched to perceive some points of similarity between the Heroic Ages of the past and our own bloodstained epoch as it moves into an increasingly bleak future, and between the bards who recited the deeds of the ancient heroes and such a novelist as Hemingway—bearing in mind the retrogressive character of our own 'heroism,' and, of course, putting the disparity between Homer and Hemingway into some proportion with that existing between, say, Hector or Agamemnon and Harry Morgan.

II

In any serious considerations of the writings of Ernest Hemingway the fact must not be lost sight of that their author belongs to that generation of men whose formative adult years were spent on the battlefields of Europe during the first world war. It would scarcely be too much to say that Hemingway's special type of outlook is *a product of the battlefield.* Hemingway's comments upon war as a subject for the writer have already been noted. And it is a revealing fact that his two most coherent and most successful books, *A Farewell to Arms* (1929) and *For Whom the Bell Tolls* (1941), upon which his fame largely rests, are both "novels of love and war."

Each of these novels stands apart from the bulk of Hemingway's work by virtue of its embodiment of a sustained pathos; and this pathos, it is evident, is an aspect of its interior connection with Hemingway's own personal experience and vision of life. While much of Hemingway's writing is the product of a somewhat uneasy attitudinizing, *A Farewell to Arms* impresses one with its surprisingly genuine and unforced quality. It is naïve rather than cynical, bewildered rather than "tough," and there is a minimum of deliberate sensational violence. Although published ten years after the end of the first world war, its clearly autobiographical character would seem to justify its being related to the early and comparatively unformed Hemingway, the Hemingway who was himself, in youthful immaturity, thrust by circumstances into the scarifying circumstances of war and left to digest his experience as best he could.

For a novelist with no coherent inner vision of human existence, the problem of form must present almost insuperable difficulties: difficulties which may be envisaged from a reading of Hemingway's two chaotic lesser novels, not considered here—*The Sun Also Rises* and *To Have and Have Not.* But in *A Farewell to Arms* this problem is solved by the exterior pattern of the events in which the curiously nameless hero is passively involved. The story is straightforward. An American enlisted in the medical section of the Italian Army, the hero meets, near the front, an English nurse called Catherine Barkley. They are indifferently attracted to one another, and there is a rather flat emotional encounter between them, very well described. (Catherine is mourning for her lover, killed in France, to whom she had put off her marriage.) Then the American is wounded and sent back to a hospital where he is nursed by Catherine, and they fall into an intimate sexual relationship. After his recovery, the American returns to the battlefront, but is involved in a disorderly retreat, is arrested and about to be shot by military police, but he frees himself, and "through" with the war, makes his way to the town where Catherine is living and escapes with her down the lakes to neutral Switzerland. Here, away from the war and in outwardly idyllic circumstances, the whole accidental, haphazard series of events reaches its meaningless, accidental conclusion with Catherine's death at the maternity hospital in giving birth to a stillborn infant.

In this novel, the war, of which the central character is a more or less acquiescent and occasionally involved onlooker, is only the background and setting for the central story of the relationship between the soldier and the nurse. There is a real suggestion of pathos in the impersonal, unimpassioned account of their forlorn, uncomprehending, tacit endeavour to maintain the illusion of the happiness and meaningfulness of their fortuitous relationship against their own deeper apprehension of lovelessness, frustration and fatality, although the emphasis is entirely on the objective occurrences, and the inward significance is never directly touched upon. The following passage will provide an example of Hemingway's honest realism in dealing with his "love interest":

We walked down the corridor. The carpet was worn. There were many doors. The manager stopped and unlocked a door and opened it.

"Here you are. A lovely room."

The small boy in buttons put the package on the table in the centre of the room. The manager opened the curtains.

"It is foggy outside," he said. The room was furnished in red plush. There were many mirrors, two chairs and a large bed with a satin coverlet. A door led to the bathroom.

"I will send up the menu," the manager said. He bowed and went out.

I went to the window and looked out, then pulled a cord that shut the thick plush curtains. Catherine was sitting on the bed, looking at the cut-glass chandelier. She had taken her hat off and her hair shone under the light. She saw herself in one of the mirrors and put her hands to her hair. She did not look happy. She let her cape fall on the bed.

"What's the matter, darling?"

"I never felt like a whore before," she said. I went over to the window and pulled the curtain aside and looked out. I had not thought it would be like this.

"You're not a whore."

"I know it, darling. But it isn't nice to feel like one." Her voice was dry and flat.

"This was the best hotel we could get in," I said. I looked out of the window. Across the square were the lights of the station. There were carriages going by on the street and I saw the trees in the park. The lights from the hotel shone on the wet pavement. Oh, hell, I thought, do we have to argue now?

"Come over here, please," Catherine said. The flatness was all gone

out of her voice. "Come over, please. I'm a good girl again." I looked
over at the bed. She was smiling.

I went over and sat on the bed beside her and kissed her.

"You're my good girl."

"I'm certainly yours," she said.

There is, too, a queer, twisted pathetic quality in the lovers' final
interview, when Catherine is on her deathbed.

"Do you want me to get a priest or anyone to come and see you?"

"Just you," she said. Then a little later, "I'm not afraid. I just hate it."

"You must not talk so much," the doctor said.

"All right," Catherine said.

"Do you want me to do anything, Cat? Can I get you anything?"

Catherine smiled, "No." Then a little later, "You won't do our things
with another girl, or say the same things, will you?"

"Never."

"I want you to have girls, though."

"I don't want them."

These short passages are enough perhaps, to make plain something
of the novel's relatively sympathetic quality. There is an absence of
deliberate harsh violence; what violence there is comes, unsought, from
the external circumstances of war, and is received passively. This is in
keeping with the character of the young man, who is not a proletarian
tough, but an average young bourgeois American. He is—not a sufferer, for although he endures suffering he refuses to accept it—but a
victim, who has not yet become hard and cynical and addicted to violence as an end in itself. If, at the beginning of the story, he has a
philosophy, it is a simple one of self-centered enjoyment, although
towards the end, and after Catherine's death, this gives place to a naïve
"tragic" outlook, which is expressed in such reflections as these:

Often a man wishes to be alone and a girl wishes to be alone too and
if they love each other they are jealous of that in each other, but I can
truly say we never felt that. We could feel alone when we were together,
alone against the others. It has only happened to me like that once. I
have been alone while I was with many girls and that is the way that
you can be most lonely. But we were never lonely and never afraid
when we were together. I know that the night is not the same as the
day: that all things are different, that the things of the night cannot be
explained in the day, because they do not then exist, and the night can
be a dreadful time for lonely people once their loneliness has started.
But with Catherine there was almost no difference in the night except
that it was an even better time. If people bring so much courage to this
world the world has to kill them to break them, so of course it kills them.
The world breaks every one and afterward many are strong in the broken
places. But these that will not break it kills. It kills the very good and

the very gentle and the very brave impartially. If you are none of these you can be sure it will kill you too but there will be no special hurry.

The harsh note of suppressed grief on which this story closes expresses the fatalistic stoicism which arises in the young American out of his inherent inner passivity as it is affected by his sense of futility and of loss. At such an intensity of suffering there are usually only two courses open to the human heart, a receptive softening or a cynical hardening. But we already know that a desperate, bitter hardness is a characteristic of Hemingway's work as a whole.

A survey of the ground covered by the greater part of Hemingway's writings shows it to be that indicated in the first part of this essay— the delineation of an eviscerated, chaotic world of futility and boredom lit up with flashes of violent action, where life is brought into a sensational vividness only by contrast with the nullity of death. The bulk of Hemingway's writing expresses consciously an outlook on life which is negative to the point of nihilism.

John Killinger: The Existential Hero

An existential interpretation will likewise answer the question of why Catherine Henry had to die in *A Farewell to Arms.*

Catherine is one of the most likely of Hemingway's women to make a Hemingway man happy and give him a maximum amount of freedom. Throughout the novel in which she appears, she is amenable to Henry's suggestions, eager to please him. She too is simple, perhaps because she is a war nurse and has herself seen much death and brutality. In the questionable hotel in Milan—the one with the red plush furnishings which made Catherine feel like a whore for seven minutes —Henry says,

> "You're a fine simple girl."
> "I am a simple girl," she replies. "No one ever understood it except you. . . . I'm a very simple girl."
> "I didn't think so at first," says Henry. "I thought you were a crazy girl."
> "I was a little crazy. But I wasn't crazy in any complicated manner."

Yet from the beginning there is a hint of complication in their alliance. When Henry, having hardly gotten to know her, invites Rinaldi to come in to see her, Rinaldi refuses, explaining that he prefers "the simpler pleasures." The simpler pleasures are those of the whorehouse, where a man pays a fee but does not become entangled. And even after Henry's farewell to arms, which harks the reader back to Nick Adams' "separate peace," he is still not, like Nick, free from a lingering feeling of guilt:

> The war was a long way away. Maybe there wasn't any war. There was no war here. Then I realized it was over for me. But I did not have the feeling that it was really over. I had the feeling of a boy who thinks of what is happening at a certain hour at the schoolhouse from which he has played truant.

It is only when the complication is intensified by the presence of Catherine and their removal to the Swiss chalet that he ceases to feel compunctions about his truancy.

"The Existential Hero." From Hemingway and the Dead Gods *by John Killinger (Lexington: University of Kentucky Press, 1960), pp. 46–48. Copyright © 1960 by the University of Kentucky Press. Reprinted by permission of the publisher.*

The extreme complication, however, the one demanding death for both the mother and the baby, is the baby itself. It is evident that the duties of fatherhood will threaten Henry's freedom. Catherine asks him, after telling him that she is pregnant, if he feels trapped. "Maybe a little," he answers. "But not by you."

"I didn't mean by me," she says. "You mustn't be stupid. I meant trapped at all."

Henry says, "You always feel trapped biologically."

The idea is not new here in Hemingway; in fact, it seems ingrained in his thinking. He, too, had come not too happily to fatherhood. And the hand of the author is unmistakable in "Cross-Country Snow," where Nick regrets that he must relinquish his skiing in the Alps with a male companion to return to the States for his wife to have a baby.

Catherine regrets the coming birth of the child, because she realizes the psychological constriction it puts upon Henry. More than once she apologizes for making trouble for him. He behaves more gracefully *in situation,* however, than the male in "Hills Like White Elephants," who wants his sweetheart to have an abortion so that they can go on as they have lived in the past, or than Richard Gordon in *To Have and Have Not,* who took his wife to "that dirty aborting horror," or than Mathieu in Sartre's *Age of Reason,* who planned, until Daniel offered to marry her, to have an abortion performed on Marcelle.

But the darkness of Catherine's death is a cloud spread by the author as a disguise for pulling off a *deus ex machina* to save his hero from the existential hell of a complicated life. Henry's philippic against the impersonal "they" that kills you—that killed Aymo gratuitously, that gave Rinaldi the syphilis, and that now is killing Catherine—is fine rhetoric and perhaps much in place for a universe without God in our time, but it is the author himself who is guilty of Catherine's death because of his fondness for the hero, and who makes a scapegoat of the world. The Henry who walks off into the rainy night at the end of *A Farewell to Arms* is like the Orestes who exists with the Furies in *Les Mouches*—he is alone, tormented, but very much alive in an existential sense.

Several critics have noted the recurrence of rain (or other forms of precipitation) in Hemingway's fiction, and especially in *A Farewell to Arms,* as a harbinger of disaster. Since it *is* connected with death, they generally agree that this function is diametrically opposite that of the precipitation symbol in the wasteland world of T. S. Eliot. But I believe that the rain is a symbol of fertility in Hemingway, too, though in a slightly different sense than in Eliot. To Hemingway death means rebirth for the existentialist hero in its presence, and therefore the rain, as an omen of death, at the same time predicts rebirth. The precipitation-death-rebirth combination is especially pertinent to the recurrent use of rain in *A Farewell to Arms* and of snow in *For Whom the Bell Tolls*; and a case might even be made for a theory that old Santiago, who is an existentialist in the grand style ("He was too simple to wonder when he had attained humility"), is an authentic individual because he is an old man *of the sea*, which is both a perennial reminder of man's finitude and a primordial womb symbol.

Norman Friedman: Small Hips, Not War

The pathetic misfortune which Frederick Henry suffers in losing Catherine through childbirth, at the end of *A Farewell to Arms*, is commonly interpreted as the result of one or the other of two causes, or some combination: he is seen either as the justly punished outlaw for having loved without benefit of clergy, or as the pitiful victim of the arbitrary and remorseless fortunes of war. Either way, what interests modern critics of this novel is, first, its portrait of a generation becoming lost in its conflict with a middle-class industrial society which it cannot accept, and second, the way this portrait suggests the wasteland archtype in its symbolic use of rain and snow, mountain and plain, lake and river, wound and love, death in birth, and so on. Thus seen, this book is taken as making a profound artistic comment on the breakdown of values in the twentieth century: the impossibility of living and loving truly while following traditional sanctions, the consequent necessity for keeping one's guard up and taking only calculated risks, and the pathos which ensues when one of the brave is caught with his guard down.[1]

Now all of this may be true in a large and general way, but even the supporters of this interpretation have sometimes felt a sense of strain in trying to reconcile the two obviously discrete portions of the book, which their punning on its title serves to point up—the "arms" of battle and the "arms" of a woman. This is clearly, as any textbook survey will tell you, "a novel of love and war," but the relationship between

"*Small Hips, Not War*" (*Editor's title*) *by Norman Friedman. From "Criticism and the Novel: Hardy, Hemingway, Crane, Woolf, Conrad,"* The Antioch Review *17: 352–55. Copyright © 1958 by Antioch Press. Reprinted by permission of Antioch Press.*

[1] Cf. J. W. Beach, *American Fiction 1920–1940* (New York, 1941), pp. 84 ff.; R. B. West, Jr. and R. W. Stallman, *The Art of Modern Fiction* (New York, 1949), pp. 622–634; Philip Young, *Ernest Hemingway* (New York, 1952), pp. 60–66; C. H. Baker, *Hemingway: the Writer as Artist* (Princeton, 1952), Ch. V; and H. K. Russell, "The Catharsis in *A Farewell to Arms*," MFS [Modern Fiction Studies], I (1955), 25–30.

the two has been taken to be largely associative and symbolic: war destroys lovers just as society destroys love, or something of the sort.

But let us see what a scrutiny of the actual events and their connections reveals. Hemingway has divided his story into five Books, and the central incidents of each may be outlined as follows:

I. Henry meets Catherine, goes into battle, and is wounded.

II. He is sent to a hospital, meets her there, and their love flowers.

III. His wound is better, he goes back to the war, is caught up in a retreat, and is forced to desert.

IV. He finds his way back to Catherine, who is bearing his child.

V. They escape to neutral territory where, after some months, she dies in childbirth.

Notice first of all the proportions devoted to each of the story's two "halves": only the last part of Book I (chs. IX–XIII) and most of Book III deal with the war directly, whereas the remaining three-and-a-half Books deal mainly with the love affair. This suggests that, perhaps because of Hemingway's skill in such writing, we might be overestimating the relative importance of war in the plot as a whole.

A further analysis of the causal connections among these Books bears out this suggestion rather clearly. Since the main culminating incident derives its force and meaning almost entirely from the relationship between the lovers, it would not be an unreasonable hypothesis to assume that the main action of the novel is organized around that relationship. We may ask first, then, what brought about this catastrophe? and secondly, what part does the war play in this sequence?

In the first place, I think it is clear that there is one sufficient cause of Catherine's death, and one only: biology ("You always feel trapped biologically"). That is, her hips were too narrow for a normal delivery —"The doctor said I was rather narrow in the hips and it's all for the best if we keep young Catherine small."—and by the time her doctor decided a caesarian was needed, the baby had strangled itself and she had developed an internal hemorrhage.

Their love for each other, and the fact that they chose to consummate their love physically, is naturally the necessary condition for this effect. But there is no reason whatever in these circumstances as such for so terrible an outcome; nothing prevented a normal delivery except Catherine's unfortunate anatomical characteristics. The same circumstances, given wider hips, could just as easily have ended in a successful delivery; and, by the same token, the same narrowness of hips could just as easily have produced the same catastrophe in the peaceful suburbs.

They could have been married fifty times over, as Henry himself reflects, and thus the theory that he suffers for daring to defy social mores will not bear up under the weight of evidence. Similarly, he could have suffered almost as much if his love had flowered in peace-time, and thus the theory that he is a victim of the war proves equally invalid. Indeed, if we speculate as to what Hemingway could have done had he wanted to do what these theories would have him do, we will see even more clearly the lack, which they ignore, of those causal connections needed. Had Hemingway wanted to make Henry suffer for violating moral conventions, for example, he could have had Catherine's death stem directly from some mischance encountered while loving immorally—she could have contracted a venereal disease from Henry, for instance, or they could have been forced to make love under physical conditions unfavorable to normal conception, and so on. But there is absolutely no hint or implication of anything like this in the narration of the final chapters. Or again, had Hemingway wanted to make Henry suffer as a victim of the war, he could have had Catherine's death result from some contingency of battle, for which any number of gruesome possibilities suggest themselves—she could have been injured while rowing across to Switzerland, or while being caught up in the retreat, or because of having to give birth without medical attention, or under unsanitary conditions, and so on. But the fact is that she had, by and large, a quiet confinement and the best medical care and facilities available. (The possibility that it is the doc-tor's fault in not operating sooner presents itself, but is not supported by the text; and even if it were, would make very little sense.)

What, then, secondly, *is* the function of the war in relation to this main action? The answer may be discussed under two heads: its causal function, and its intensifying function. Causally, although the war is a sufficient condition of neither their love nor their suffering which is the outcome of this love, it does serve as a necessary condition of this love. Without it, they in all probability would never have met, and even if they had, Catherine would have still had her English fiancé. But the war, in simply bringing them together in a susceptible mood, would not in itself have thrown them in love. Indeed, Catherine met Rinaldi first without being attracted to him at all. The sufficient cause of the love between Henry and Catherine stems primarily from their respec-tive characters and attitudes. The war, further, inflicts a wound upon Henry, which in turn allows him to see more of Catherine and thus to consummate their love; and again, by means of the retreat, the war allows him to return to her and thus to be in attendance when her time arrives. But in each case, its functional role is that of a necessary condition rather than that of a sufficient cause.

Frederick J. Hoffman: The Secret Wound

One of the most radical changes in modern literary sensibility can be described as the symbolic injury. The circumstances of such an injury are almost invariably violent, and the violence, while not entirely unexpected, comes as a surprise, as a shock, to the person injured. There are some evidences of security even here, though quite superficial and not at the heart of the experience. The hero may be with soldiers whom he knows, with whom he talks and eats an improvised meal. Beyond this scene, there are the love and the religion he has left. About him there are many threatening noises, and these bear promise of violent injury or death. If one of these noises should come near, to actualize the danger, that is an accident; but the accident is the result not of mere chance but of impersonal misfortune impersonally caused. The injury, when it comes, is a form of death whether the victim survives it or not.

Hemingway once spoke of his own injury, on the night of July 8th, 1918, as a death[1] (it is important too that the injury should occur at night). "I died then," he is reported by Malcolm Cowley as having said, "I felt my soul or something coming right out of my body, like you'd pull a silk handkerchief out of a pocket by one corner. It flew around and then came back and went in again and I wasn't dead any more!" [2] According to Ezra Pound's version, told to John Peale Bishop, Hemingway "had lain four days under the debris of the trench" before he was rescued; this, adds Bishop, "is one day longer underground than Lazarus." Though the facts of this account may not be true, they do have a symbolic meaning: Hemingway's "awareness of death," his experience of it, had led to a form of rebirth, had "separated" him from his (as well as from Nick Adams') American past, from the Middle West. The experience of the wound and the circumstances in which it had happened radically altered Hemingway's entire view of the world he re-entered. He had therefore to find different perspective from which to view and judge the world.

"*The Secret Wound*" (*Editor's title*). *From* The Twenties: American Writing in the Postwar Decade by *Frederick J. Hoffman* (*New York: The Viking Press, Inc., 1955*), *pp. 67–72. Copyright 1955 by Frederick J. Hoffman. Reprinted by permission of the publisher.*

[1] He was with three Italian soldiers at the time; all three of them died. Hemingway was himself all but given up for dead—237 fragments of the "Minnie" shell were extracted from one leg alone.

[2] Cf. *A Farewell to Arms:* "I went out swiftly, all of myself, and I knew I was dead and that it had all been a mistake to think you just died."

The most important consequence of a traumatic shock is that the experience that caused it is recalled again and again. It is not that the victim enjoys the experience and so wishes it repeated, but rather that initially it has thrown him entirely off balance and he is therefore unable to adjust to it.[3] The more violent and unexpected the experience, the more liable it is to such compulsive repetition, which is in reality a long and painful means of reaching a stage of complete adjustment. A severe injury to the body suggests a comparably severe injury to the psychic nature. The injured man will not rest until he has found what is to him a meaningful and original pattern of adjustment. The shock often has other effects: for one, it may upset his confidence in the past —his own past and the social past of which he has been a part. The experience is itself almost equivalent to a death; what follows it amounts to a new and a different life. The man who survives violence is often quite remarkably different from the man who has never experienced it.

The symbolic wound has affected a large share of Hemingway's fiction. Its distinguishing features are the shock of the actual occurrence, the sudden cutting away of past experience and securities (which do survive, but only in fragmentary form), the mystery and impersonality of its source, the anger, fear, and helplessness that are part of the reaction to it. The wound is "unreasonable"; that is, the victim cannot understand why "it has happened to *him*." It gives him a profound distrust of those who—remote from the experience itself—try to formulate explanations or assurances about it. They are obviously "faking"; they don't know what they are talking about; if they knew what it was really like, they would not talk at all, and they would most certainly not try to speak of dignty or glory or sacrifice, because these words are almost invariably betrayed when tested by reality. But some definition of a man's life is necessary if he is to care about surviving, and this definition is hard to formulate when so many useful words and expressions have defaulted. . . .

A Farewell to Arms contains the fullest account of this kind of death. Lieutenant Henry is wounded in terms roughly similar to Hemingway's actual experience. Very important too are certain facts of the novel's war setting: Gorizia, the "nice" town, with its hospitals, its cafés, its two brothels (one reserved for the officers), its artillery up side streets. Dominating the town are the artillery pieces, which in the summer are "covered with green branches" to disguise them as part of the landscape.[4] In the mountains, at the front, they are hidden from view,

---

[3] Cf. Sigmund Freud, *Beyond the Pleasure Principle* (1922); see Philip Young, *Ernest Hemingway* (1953).

[4] Note also the troops, who wore cartridge boxes under their capes, so that they looked "as though they were six months gone with child"—death masquerading as life; the battlefront "no place for virgins" or for mothers.

and only the round puffs of smoke can be seen: "You saw the flash, then heard the crack, then saw the smoke ball distort and thin in the wind." The two important ministers to the faith and security of the soldiers are the priest and Rinaldi the surgeon. The guns, the surgeon, and the brothels all act to reduce life at the front to its secular minimum; the priest is always "five against one," as the Captain says at the officers' mess. The priest's advice is rarely taken seriously; his remarks are not quite like the patriotic phrases of the battle police, but they are heard by Lieutenant Henry with embarrassment, and sometimes with boredom.

The most crucial of all Hemingway's explorations of the military condition is his description of the retreat from Caporetto (Book Three). The retreat begins in an orderly enough fashion, but as it proceeds the sense of order dissolves. It becomes "unreasonable"; Italians fire on Italians; Germans break through the lines, the *carabinieri* suspect impartially and kill the innocent. In the landscape of unreason of which this section of the novel gives a brilliant description, Lieutenant Henry loses all sense of personal dedication to his fellow soldiers, abandons his feeling of responsibility to the army, and breaks out of the trap the war has laid for him. From then on he links his fate with only a few persons—nurses, doctors, and bartenders—and they serve his emotional needs and protect him from dangers.

This does not, however, save him from ultimate defeat; it is important to see his defeat in terms of the "unreasonable wound" received earlier. The death of Catherine Barkley, however remote its setting from that of the war, is placed in sharp equation with the defeating and confusing terror of the war itself. The long, slow, almost monotonous life of waiting in Switzerland intensifies the terror and bitterness of the final scene. The two deaths of that scene are an excruciating addition to the evidence of impersonal cruelty the novel as a whole provides. The child is stillborn and the mother dies in her attempt to give him life. Here there is no priest to speak of God and love; there are only death and the rain outside on the walk back to the hotel. Catherine's death is another example of the unreasonable wound, more pathetic really because it defeats a plan to which Lieutenant Henry has irrevocably committed himself.

A Farewell to Arms affords a remarkably complete view of the modern death about which Miss Cather was so critical. Superficially, Lieutenant Henry may be said to have had an honorable choice of two equally persuasive and practicable modes of action. Actually, the choices are neither persuasive nor practicable. The war itself gives only one kind of answer to the questions posed by those living at its center: the shock, the surprise, the helpless anger are present three times in the novel—when Lieutenant Henry is wounded, at the end of the re-

treat, and in Catherine's death in Switzerland. The setting of the war
—the guns hidden in the mountains and dealing impersonally in death
—dominates Hemingway's fiction throughout the postwar decade. To
this specter priest, surgeon, and other men of skill or good intention
pay futile and desperate heed, but adjustment to the violent and in-
calculable death which is its gift cannot be made with the help of any
of them.

Leslie Fiedler: Love and Death

In Hemingway the rejection of the sentimental happy ending of
marriage involves the acceptance of the sentimental happy beginning
of innocent and inconsequential sex, camouflages the rejection of ma-
turity and of fatherhood itself. The only story in which he portrays a
major protagonist as having a child is the one in which he remembers
with nostalgia his little Trudy of the "well holding arms, quick searching tongue," and looks forward to the time when his son will have a
gun and they can pop off to the forest like two boys together. More
typically he aspires to be not Father but "Papa," the Old Man of the
girl-child with whom he is temporarily sleeping; and surely there is no
writer to whom childbirth more customarily presents itself as the essential catastrophe. At best he portrays it as a plaguey sort of accident
which forces a man to leave his buddies behind at the moment of
greatest pleasure as in "Cross Country Snow"; at worst, it becomes in
his fiction that horror which drives the tender-hearted husband of
"Indian Camp" to suicide, or which takes Catherine away from Lieutenant Henry in *A Farewell to Arms*. Poor things, all they wanted was
innocent orgasm after orgasm on an island of peace in a world at war,
love-making without end in a scarcely real country to which neither
owed life or allegiance.

But such a relationship can, of course, never last, as Hemingway-
Nick Adams-Lieutenant Henry has always known: "They all ended
the same. Long time ago good. Now no good." Only the dead woman
becomes neither a bore nor a mother; and before Catherine can quite
become either she must die, killed not by Hemingway, of course, but
by childbirth! It is all quite sad and lovely at the end: the last kiss
bestowed on what was a woman and is now a statue, the walk home
through the rain. Poe himself could not have done better, though he

"Love and Death." From Love and Death in the American Novel *by Leslie
Fiedler (New York: Stein and Day Publishers, 1966), pp. 317–18. Copyright ©
1966, 1960 by Leslie A. Fiedler. Reprinted by permission of Stein and Day Publishers and Jonathan Cape Ltd.*

was haunted not by the memory of a plump little Indian on the hemlock needles but a fantasy of a high-born maiden "loved with a love that was more than love" and carried away by death. In an odd way Hemingway's Trudy and Poe's Annabel Lee are sisters under the skin, projections both of a refusal to surrender the innocence of childhood —to leave seashore or woodland Eden where child loves child: projections both of the desire for death!

Had Catherine lived, she could only have turned into a bitch; for this is the fate in Hemingway's imagination of all Anglo-Saxon women. In him, the cliché of Dark Lady and Fair survives, but stood on its head, exactly reversed. The Dark Lady, who is neither wife nor mother, blends with the image of Fayaway, the exotic servant-consort reconstructed by Melville in *Typee* out of memories of an eight-year-old Polynesian girl-child. In Hemingway, such women are mindless, soft, subservient; painless devices for extracting seed without human engagement. The Fair Lady, on the other hand, who gets pregnant and wants a wedding, or uses her sexual allure to assert her power, is seen as a threat and a destroyer of men. But the seed-extractors are Indians or Latins, black-eyed and dusky in hue, while the castrators are at least Anglo-Saxon if not symbolically blond. Neither are permitted to be virgins; indeed, both are imagined as having been often possessed, though in the case of the Fair Woman promiscuity is used as a device for humiliating and unmanning the male foolish enough to have entered into a marriage with her. Through the Dark anti-virgin, on the other hand, a new lover enters into a blameless communion with the other uncommitted males who have possessed her and departed, as well as with those yet to come. It is a kind of homosexuality once-removed, the appeal of the whorehouse (Eden of the world of men without women) embodied in a single figure.

Edgar Johnson: Farewell the Separate Peace

. . . In *A Farewell to Arms* it is society as a whole that is rejected, social responsibility, social concern. Lieutenant Henry is in the War, but his attitude toward it is purely that of a spectator, refusing to be involved. He is leading a private life as an isolated individual. Even personal relations, of any depth or intimacy, he avoids; he drinks with the officers and talks with the priest and visits the officers' brothel, but

"Farewell the Separate Peace" by Edgar Johnson. From Sewanee Review *48* (*1940*): *289–90.* Copyright © *1940* by Edgar Johnson. *Reprinted by permission of the* Sewanee Review.

all contacts he keeps, deliberately, on a superficial level. He has rejected the world.

Such an attitude is possible only to a sensitive and reflective person. Henry is no naïve barbarian. He was studying architecture in Italy when the War began; he makes ironical remarks about sculptures and bronzes; his reflections and conversation contain allusions to Samuel Johnson, Saint Paul, Andrew Marvell, and Sir Thomas Wyatt. His flight from responsibility is the ultimate of the flight that Jake and Brett and Mike were trying to effect with drink and bullfights and sex. He is evading responsibility and emotion, taking refuge in simple primary sensations. Successfully, so far as the War is concerned: "I was always embarrassed by the words sacred, glorious and sacrifice and the expression in vain. . . . Abstract words, such as glory, honor, courage, or hallow were obscene beside the concrete names of villages, the number of roads, the names of rivers, the numbers of regiments and the dates."

It is hardly possible to miss the intensity here trying to masquerade as a hardboiled indifference, endeavoring to shore itself against the immeasurable cruelty of things and the callous glibness of words. Even more than Jake, Henry is immuring himself in an ivory tower of trying not to feel. But an indifference preserved in the face of such underlying emotion is precariously held. It breaks down upon his meeting with Catherine Barkley.

"God knows I had not wanted to fall in love with her. I had not wanted to fall in love with any one." Emotion has found an entering wedge, although Henry tries even now to draw a circle enclosing themselves alone. The world without is the enemy. "Because there's only us two and in the world there's all the rest of them," Catherine says. "If anything comes between us we're gone and they have us." Henry deserts, he escapes to Switzerland with Catherine. He no longer even reads about the fighting. "I was going to forget the war. I had made a separate peace." (So the dying boy in one of the interchapters of *In Our Time* whispers to his fatally wounded comrade, "You and me, we've made a separate peace.") But momentarily Hemingway tries to ignore the implication that the only separate peace is in death. He will solve the problem of dealing with the world by taking refuge in individualism and isolated personal relationships and sensations. He too will make a separate peace.

But the separate peace soon turns out to be impossible. Hemingway's honesty and understanding will not allow him to pretend it is successful. Catherine undergoes a prolonged and painful childbirth, and ultimately she dies. "You did not know what it was all about. You never had time to learn. They threw you in and told you the rules and the first time they caught you off base they killed you." In the end, then, one could not be a candle-holder and look on. Life caught you up, willy-nilly, by your instincts, by your sensations, by your emotions, caught you in a trap; and the better you were the harder it dealt with you. "If people bring so much courage to the world the world has to kill them to break them, so of course it kills them. . . . It kills the very good and the very gentle and the very grave impartially. If you are none of these you can be sure it will kill you too but there will be no special hurry."

Such is the result of trying to reject society and reject responsibility. It seemed to lead back with intensified bitterness to the vision of cosmic cruelty underlying *In Our Time*. Life was only an endless abrasion and destruction, even more harsh to the intelligent and the good than to all the others. To them it brings "only the remorseless devaluation of nature . . . which bears away of our great hopes, emotions, and ambitions only a few and soon disintegrating trifles." The end of the road was blank disheartenment, despair for life and civilization and mankind.

Maxwell Geismar: The Human Will

> He did not like them when he saw them in the Greek's ice cream parlor. He did not want them themselves really. They were too complicated. . . . He did not want to get into the intrigue and the politics. He did not want to have to do any more courting. He did not want to tell any more lies. It wasn't worth it. . . . He did not want any consequences. He did not want any consequences ever again. He wanted to live along without consequences.

Nowhere more clearly than in the story of Krebs has Hemingway given us his underlying attitude—this living along without consequences, the emotional withdrawal from experience and moral renunciation of life's responsibilities; this looking at things henceforth from a variety of porches rather than participating in all the streets of life. And "A Farewell to Arms," four years after Krebs, gives the unified history of the events which led up to such a conclusion.

Returning to read the famous novel after all the prefaces by Parisian bohemians like Ford Madox Ford, and the excitement of the American popular reception, is, I believe, still a fine experience. For the book is without doubt as fresh today as in 1929, as gay and moving. Against the gaiety, the warmth of "A Farewell to Arms," Hemingway portrays, of course, the cumulative degeneration of the human temperament under the conditions of war. The novel is a series of human defeats within one continuous and terrible sequence: the rains, the cholera, the soldiers who mutilate themselves rather than go on fighting, the growing weariness of the Italian army which led up to Caporetto, the degeneration of Rinaldi himself who is symptomatic of the novel's pattern, and at its start is so quick and alive. Contrasted against this in turn, in the love of Lieutenant Henry and Catherine Barkley we have another antithesis of increasing joy. The love and the despair are constantly related, intensely intertwined, and in the end almost gain the feeling of life and death themselves: the death preying upon the living organism of the lovers' hope, eating into the flesh and destroying the form from page to page. Yet each change of form, each advance of destruction makes the life of the novel more vital, the life we know must yield, but in the manner of its yielding asserting itself beyond its destruction.

"A Farewell to Arms" in this sense lies quite outside of the pattern of Hemingway's development which we have been showing. For the feeling of tragedy in the novel comes precisely from the struggle to participate in life despite all the odds, from the efforts of the lovers to fulfill themselves in a sterile world, from the exact impact of the human will which Hemingway has negated. Yet even here we must notice that Lieutenant Henry turns his back upon our society after Caporetto. Following his personal objectives he abandons his friends, his responsibilities as an officer, the entire complex of organized social life represented by the army and the war. This farewell to arms is accomplished without request or permission. Lieutenant Henry, in fact, deserts, and his action is prophetic of his author's own future movement. "You and me," says Nick to the Rinaldi of "In Our Time," "we've made a separate peace." And Hemingway's separate peace was to embrace the woods of Michigan as well as Caporetto, the activities of normal times as well as war, and even at last the ordinary purposes of the individual's life within his society, as well as the collective purposes of society as a whole.

Chronology of Important Dates

	Hemingway	The Age
1899	Hemingway born, Oak Park, Illinois.	
1912		Pound, influenced by T. E. Hulme, launches Imagism.
1915		Pound's letter to Harriet Marlowe.
1917	Graduates from Oak Park High School. Army rejects him for eye injury from boxing; becomes reporter for Kansas City *Star*.	United States enters World War I against Germany.
1918	Becomes Red Cross ambulance driver, Norton-Harjes Corps. Wounded in the legs near Fossalta di Piave.	Treaty of Brest-Litovsk; Allies and Central Powers sign Armistice.
1919		Versailles Treaty. T. S. Eliot's essays, "Tradition and the Individual Talent," and "Hamlet and His Problems."
1920		League of Nations established; United States rejection of Versailles Treaty.
1920–24	Foreign correspondent for Toronto *Star*.	
1921	Marries Hadley Richardson; settles in Europe.	
1922	Introduced to Gertrude Stein, Ezra Pound, James Joyce, Ford Madox Ford.	T. S. Eliot, *The Wasteland*. Mussolini's march on Rome.
1923	*Three Stories and Ten Poems* published in Paris.	

1924	*In Our Time* published in Paris.	Ford Madox Ford edits *Transatlantic Review*; T. E. Hulme, *Speculations*.
1925		Treaties of Locarno. T. S. Eliot, "The Hollow Men."
1926	*The Sun Also Rises* published in New York.	
1927	Divorces Hadley; marries Pauline Pfeiffer. Publishes *Men Without Women*.	
1928	Begins *A Farewell to Arms*. Son, Patrick, born. Father, Dr. Clarence Hemingway, commits suicide. Continues *A Farewell to Arms* at Key West, Florida; Piggott, Arkansas; Kansas City, Missouri. Completes first draft at Big Horn, Sheridan County, Wyoming.	
1929	Completes revision of *A Farewell to Arms*. Novel serialized in *Scribner's Magazine*. Novel published in New York.	United States stock market crash.
1930–35		The Great Depression.
1932	*Death in the Afternoon*.	
1933	Hunts in Africa.	Hitler becomes German Chancellor.
1934	*Green Hills of Africa*.	
1936	Campaigns in support of Spanish Loyalists.	Spanish Civil War begins.
1937	Covers the war in Spain for North American Newspaper Alliance. Publishes *To Have and Have Not*.	
1939		Surrender of Madrid; Germany invades Poland.
1940	*For Whom the Bell Tolls*. Divorced by Pauline Pfeiffer; marries Martha Gellhorn.	

1941		Japanese attack on Pearl Harbor; U.S. enters World War II.
1942–45	*Men at War.* Free-Lance correspondent in the European theater.	
1944	Divorce from Martha Gellhorn; marries Mary Walsh.	
1945		Surrender of Germany and Japan; end of World War II.
1950	*Across the River and Into the Trees.*	
1951	*The Old Man and the Sea.*	
1952		Batista becomes military dictator of Cuba.
1954	Awarded Nobel Prize for Literature, ". . . mastery of the art of modern narration."	
1959	Covers the duel of matadors Ordoñez and Dominguin.	Castro occupies Havana.
1960	*The Dangerous Summer.*	
1961	Dies of self-inflicted, possibly accidental, gunshot wound in Ketchum, Idaho.	

Notes on the Editor and Contributors

JAY GELLENS teaches at San Diego State College. He is the author of *Blind Man on the Corner*, which won the William Morris Award for Best Play of the Year at the Yale Drama School.

CARLOS BAKER is the author of critical as well as biographical studies of Hemingway. He is Professor of Literature at Princeton University.

MALCOLM COWLEY is the author of *Blue Juniata, Exile's Return*, and numerous studies of contemporary American fiction.

LESLIE FIEDLER is the influential author of *Love and Death in the American Novel* and teaches English at the Buffalo campus of the State University of New York.

NORMAN FRIEDMAN teaches at the University of Connecticut and is the author of *E. E. Cummings: The Art of His Poetry*.

MAXWELL GEISMAR is a historian of the novel and has published, among numerous other works, *Writers in Crisis, Last of the Provincials*, and *Rebels and Ancestors*.

E. M. HALLIDAY, formerly a professor at North Carolina State College, is an editor of *American Heritage*. He is the author of *Ignorant Armies*.

FREDERICK J. HOFFMAN was Professor of Literature at the University of Wisconsin and the University of California at Riverside and the author of *Perspectives on Modern Literature*.

EDGAR JOHNSON is Professor of English at the City College of New York and is the author of *Charles Dickens: His Tragedy and Triumph*.

JOHN KILLINGER, the author of *Hemingway and the Dead Gods* and *The Failure of Theology in Modern Literature*, teaches Christianity and Literature at Kentucky Southern College.

ROBERT LEWIS is an English professor at the University of Texas and has written numerous articles on modern fiction, notably "Analyzing a Novel."

WYNDHAM LEWIS was a critic and political controversialist and the author of *Men Without Art*.

Louis L. Martz is Professor of English at Yale and winner of the Christian Gauss Award for his study of seventeenth-century poetry, *The Poetry of Meditation.*

Earl Rovit is the author of *Herald to Chaos* and teaches English at the University of Louisville.

D. S. Savage is a poet and critic. Among his books are *The Personal Principle* and *The Withered Branch.*

Ray B. West, Jr., teaches at San Francisco State College and is coeditor with R. W. Stallman of *The Art of Modern Fiction.*

Philip Young is Professor of English at Pennsylvania State University and is the author of *Ernest Hemingway: A Reconsideration.*

Selected Bibliography

Atkins, John, *The Art of Ernest Hemingway: His Work and Personality*. London: Spring Books, Inc., 1952. Focuses on the events of the author's life and the way in which his writing transforms them.

Baker, Sheridan, *Ernest Hemingway: Introduction and Interpretation*. New York: Barnes & Noble, Inc., 1967. Analysis of the Hemingway hero as the "undefeated loser."

Cooperman, Stanley, "Death and Cojones: Hemingway's *A Farewell to Arms*," *South Atlantic Quarterly* 63 (Winter 1964): 85–92.

Fenton, Charles A., *The Apprenticeship of Ernest Hemingway*. New York: Farrar, Straus & Young, Inc., 1952. An extremely detailed study dealing with the early life, including World War I experiences, and the early quest for style.

Halliday, E. M., "Hemingway's Narrative Perspective," *Sewanee Review* 60 (Spring 1952): 202–18. Studies Hemingway's use of various points of view in the stories and novels.

Hotchner, A. E., *Papa Hemingway: A Personal Memoir*. New York: Random House, Inc., 1966. Informative account of Hemingway's own recollections of the events surrounding the composition of his books.

Hovey, Richard B., *Inward Terrain*. Seattle: University of Washington Press, 1968. Freudian study of the Hemingway vision.

Levin, Harry, "Observations on the Style of Ernest Hemingway," *Kenyon Review* 13 (Autumn 1951): 581–609. A suggestive analysis of Hemingway's poetic style.

TWENTIETH CENTURY
INTERPRETATIONS

MAYNARD MACK, *Series Editor*
Yale University

NOW AVAILABLE
Collections of Critical Essays
ON

ADVENTURES OF HUCKLEBERRY FINN
ALL FOR LOVE
THE AMBASSADORS
ARROWSMITH
AS YOU LIKE IT
BLEAK HOUSE
THE BOOK OF JOB
THE CASTLE
CORIOLANUS
DOCTOR FAUSTUS
DON JUAN
DUBLINERS
THE DUCHESS OF MALFI
ENDGAME
EURIPIDES' ALCESTIS
THE FALL OF THE HOUSE OF USHER
A FAREWELL TO ARMS
THE FROGS
GRAY'S ELEGY
THE GREAT GATSBY
GULLIVER'S TRAVELS
HAMLET
HARD TIMES
HENRY IV, PART TWO
HENRY V
THE ICEMAN COMETH
JULIUS CAESAR
KEATS'S ODES
LIGHT IN AUGUST

(continued on next page)

(continued from previous page)

Lord Jim
Major Barbara
Measure for Measure
The Merchant of Venice
Moll Flanders
Much Ado about Nothing
The Nigger of the "Narcissus"
Oedipus Rex
The Old Man and the Sea
Pamela
The Playboy of the Western World
The Portrait of a Lady
A Portrait of the Artist as a Young Man
The Praise of Folly
Pride and Prejudice
The Rape of the Lock
The Rime of the Ancient Mariner
Robinson Crusoe
Romeo and Juliet
Samson Agonistes
The Scarlet Letter
Sir Gawain and the Green Knight
Songs of Innocence and of Experience
Sons and Lovers
The Sound and the Fury
The Tempest
Tess of the D'Urbervilles
Tom Jones
Twelfth Night
Utopia
Vanity Fair
Walden
The Waste Land
Women in Love
Wuthering Heights